LAURIE'S SIXPENNY MANUALS OF INSTRUCTION

IN GRAMMAR—ANALYSIS—COMPOSITION—ETYMOLOGY—SPELLING—GEOGRAPHY—HISTORY—ARITHMETIC—ALGEBRA—NATURAL PHILOSOPHY—MAGNETISM—PHYSIOLOGY—POLITICAL ECONOMY—LATIN—GERMAN.

THE Editor's aim in producing this Series of cheap Manuals has been to furnish an easy Introduction to all those subjects which are now regarded as an essential part of an educational course.

The difficulty of properly fulfilling such a task—of satisfying the combined requirements of simplicity and comprehensiveness—is, as practical teachers well know, not an inconsiderable one. A crude summary of dry facts, without reason or explanation, no longer satisfies the demands of the age. Yet it is certain that instruction of a scientific kind, if it is to be effective, must be imparted step by step on a rigidly *methodical* plan.

In accordance with this principle, the SIXPENNY MANUALS OF INSTRUCTION are specially characterized by a systematic arrangement of brief Lessons (with accompanying Exercises), each of which, as it is fully mastered by the pupil, will lead naturally and easily to the next.

In short, the Editor has endeavoured in this, as in his other Rudimentary Courses, to provide a means whereby the learner, whether under a teacher or not, may at once be prepared for, and encouraged to pursue, his studies in works of higher pretensions.

LAURIE'S SIXPENNY MANUALS OF INSTRUCTION.

WITH

NUMEROUS ILLUSTRATIONS AND EXERCISES.

1. English Grammar Simplified (New Edition).
2. Explanatory English Grammar.
3. Outlines of Grammatical Analysis.
4. Easy Steps in English Composition.
5. First Steps in Etymology.
6. Webster's Guide to English Spelling.
7. Outlines of Geography (Political).
8. Sixpenny Geography (Political).
9. Outlines of Physical Geography.
10. Compendium of English History.
11. Outlines of English History.
12. Sixpenny Manual of Arithmetic. Answers,1s.
13. Rudiments of Algebra, inclnding ANSWERS.
14. Elementary Algebra. Answers, 6d.
15. Elements of Magnetism and Electricity.
16. Rudiments of Natural Philosophy.
17. Compendium of Political Economy.
18. Rudiments of Animal Physiology.
19. German Grammar and First Reader.
20. Latin Grammar and Syntax.
21. Selections of Standard Poetry.

CENTRAL SCHOOL DEPÔT, 22, PATERNOSTER ROW,
LONDON, E.C.

INFANT EDUCATION.

Descriptive Notes

ON THE

KINDERGARTEN SYSTEM.

EDITED BY J. S. LAURIE,

Formerly H.M. Inspector of Schools, etc.

SIXPENCE.

London :

THE CENTRAL SCHOOL-DEPÔT,

22, PATERNOSTER ROW, E.C. ;

SIMPKIN & CO. ; HAMILTON & CO. ; KENT & CO. ; AND ALL THE SCHOOL SOCIETIES.

"Education is a primary necessity of man. It is by education' that the organs of the body acquire accuracy in their movements. The senses of sight, hearing, taste, and smell all *learn* to act. And the earliest charm of infant life is to observe the progress of the education of the senses; to watch the study of a toy; to see the hands holding it at various distances, turning its different sides to view, tasting it, shaking it, and finally, when a little older, breaking it to see whence comes the noise. Who that has watched this process has not learned the first accomplishment of a teacher—to promote the education of the senses by the association of physical exercise, amusement, and study? The passage from infancy to childhood is but an imperceptible step, marked by the continued expressions of new experiences. Everything excites new impressions; everything must be examined with due deliberation—no hurry, no pressure, no fatigue. And during the while—ay, even during the whole period of waking hours—there is incessant motion. Nature has implanted in the young of all animals a pleasure in exercise, muscular action being not only necessary for strengthening the muscles, but also the bones to which they are attached. The actions of crying and laughing, the deep inspirations of sobbing and joy, both alike tend to develop and strengthen the lungs; and the active exercise of the lungs promotes and develops the action of the heart, which with increasing vigour sends the blood to every part of the body. In all this the brain participates to an extraordinary degree, requiring that the young mind be exercised with the utmost care. By experience and habit the child acquires judgment, learns to compare one movement with another, to direct its organs to special objects, to produce this or that action, to take this or that attitude for the accomplishment of its purposes; and all the subsequent capacity of the brain will greatly depend upon the care with which it is cultured during the period of growth. Imagination, perception, and memory, faculties which are always preceded and determined by the sensations, are all the subjects of education, enlarged and extended in proportion as new excitements and impressions call them forth and give them application."—DR. BELL.

GENERAL VIEW
OF
THE KINDERGARTEN SYSTEM.*

———◆———

Fundamental Principle of Education.—It is a truth now universally recognized by educators, that ideas are formed in the mind of a child by abstraction and generalization from the facts revealed to him through the senses ; that only what he himself has perceived of the visible and tangible properties of things can serve as the basis of thought, and that upon the vividness and completeness of the impressions made upon him by external objects will depend the clearness of his inferences and the correctness of his judgments. It is equally true, and as generally recognized, that in young children the perceptive faculties are relatively stronger than at any later period, and that while the understanding and reason still sleep the sensitive mind is receiving those sharp impressions of external things, which, held fast by memory, transformed by the imagination, and finally classified and organized through reflection, result in the determination of thought and the formation of character.

These two parallel truths indicate clearly that the first duty of the educator is to aid the perceptive faculties in their work by supplying the external objects best calculated to serve as the basis of normal conceptions, by exhibiting these objects from many different stand-points,

* A remarkably lucid and logical exposition of Fröbel's method, theoretical and practical, by Miss S. E. BLOW (Steiger, New York).

that variety of interest may sharpen and intensify the impressions they make upon the mind, and by presenting them in such a sequence that the transition from one object to another may be made as easy as possible.

Fröbel's Solution.—The advocates of the Kindergarten believe that Fröbel has met this fundamental necessity in education better than any other thinker, and that the series of objects technically called Fröbel's Gifts offer the healthiest nourishment yet discovered for the child's mind, and constitute the best basis yet known for strong and harmonious development of the intellectual powers. It is my purpose briefly to describe these gifts in the order of their succession, to indicate their connection, and to try to make clear the law by which their sequence is determined.

I. THE GIFTS.

First Gift.—Recognizing clearly the necessity of a definite starting-point for thought, Fröbel presents to the child in his first gift the *ball*, an object containing, under the simplest form, the properties common to all things. By means of the ball we illustrate the general properties of size, colour, form, weight, and density, while at the same time we give the child the easiest thing in the world to grasp alike with the hand and the mind. It is the *simplest* of forms, for it has neither sides, corners, nor edges. It is easy to conceive as a *whole*, for in all positions it appears the same.

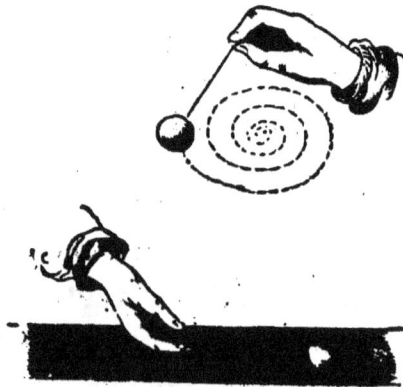

It is the *fundamental* form throughout nature, and is constantly appearing both in the organic and inorganic worlds; and, finally, it is perfectly *harmonious*, being, one might almost say, the ideal form towards which the universe strives. To the child, moreover, the ball is a source of infinitely varied amusement. He rolls it, he tosses it, he whirls it round and round. Holding it by a string, he moves it up and down, right and left, or round and round in an ever-widening or an ever-narrowing circle. It becomes to him the representative of a thousand things; through its form it stands for the fruits and flowers he has learned to love; through the motions he gives it, it becomes to him the springing cat, the flying bird, the climbing squirrel—all the objects with which his little experience of life has made him familiar are embodied in it; and just from its great simplicity result its manifold adaptations.

As introduced into the Kindergarten, the first gift consists of a box containing six soft worsted balls of the different primary and secondary colours. These balls should be so used that the child will learn through actual experience all their essential characteristics, both in rest and in motion, in their relation to each other, and in their relation to himself.

Second Gift.—The second gift, which consists of a *hard ball, a cube, and a cylinder,* involves at its basis recognition of the truth, that in order to attain clear knowledge there must be comparison, or, in other words, that we only learn what a thing *is* by learning what it *is not*. Therefore, to complete the child's knowledge of the ball, he must compare it with something else, and as his powers are too weak to discern *slight* divergences, he needs an object which well presents the most obvious possible contrast.

This we find in the cube.   Instead of the *unity* of the ball, we have in the cube *variety;* instead of the *simplicity* of the ball, we have in the cube *complexity;* instead of the unvarying *uniformity* of the ball, we have in the cube an object which changes with every modification of position, and every acceleration of movement; instead of the ready *movableness* of the ball we have in the cube an object which, as it were, embodies the notion of *rest*.

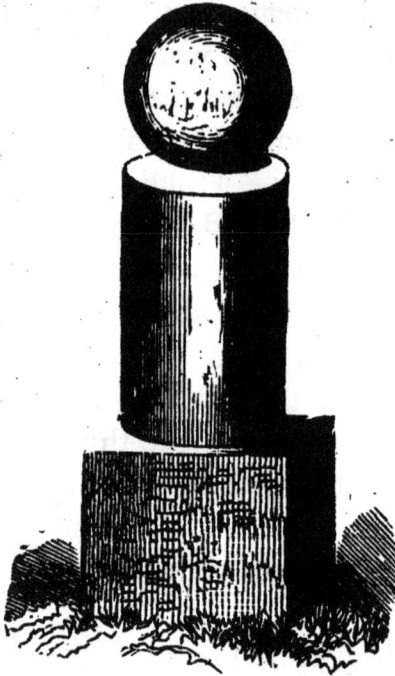

The cylinder forms the connecting link *between* the ball and the cube. Like the ball, it is round and without corners, and, like the cube, it has sides and edges. It contains the ball, and is contained by the cube, and it unites the movableness of the one with the fixedness of the other.

Third Gift.—In the third gift, which consists of a *cube divided* once in every direction, giving eight smaller cubes, we pass from contrasts of form to contrasts of size. This gift, considered as a whole, is identical with the cube of the second gift; but its divisions, enabling the child to grasp inner conditions as well as external appearance, lead from the conception of a simple unit to the elements of which such unit is composed, thus paving the way

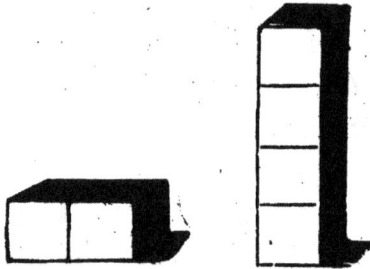

for rational analysis. And as all analysis should end with synthesis, every division of the cube into its parts is followed either by their recombination into the original whole, or by the production of a new whole, of which each small cube becomes an essential part. Thus the third gift meets the instinctive craving of the child to find out *what is inside* of things ; and at the same time, through the number and variety of its possible transformations, it satisfies and stimulates the creative powers. This gift is also excellently adapted to give children definite ideas of number, and only those who have seen the little calculators making all possible combinations of their eight cubes can understand how the experiences thus obtained will simplify arithmetic, and make it a pleasure instead of a torture alike to teacher and pupil.

Fourth Gift.—The fourth gift, like the third, is a *divided cube,* but in its subdivision we have blocks whose sides are oblongs instead of squares. And whereas, in the small cubes of the third gift, the length, breadth, and thickness were equal, the parallelopipeds of the fourth gift are twice as long as they are broad, and twice as broad as they are thick. Thus the three dimensions of space implied in the third gift are emphasized in the fourth, and all the possibilities latent in the former are actualized in the latter.

Fifth Gift.—As all development moves from the simple to the complex, and as in the child what is new unfolds from the old, so in the Kindergarten gifts which are intended to be an objective counterpart of this sub-

jective process, we find each new gift contains all that
existed in the previous gifts, with the addition of elements
which they implied but did not realise. Thus, in the
fifth gift we again have the cube—but this time the
cube is larger, the number of its parts is greatly in-

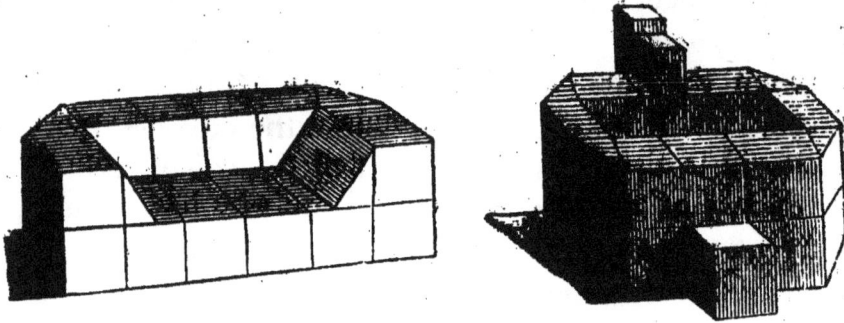

creased, and, by dividing some of the smaller cubes, the
triangular form is introduced. A greatly increased amount
of material is thus put into the hands of the child ; and
alike in extended numerical relations, in variety of fundamental forms, and in adaptability to creative purposes,
this gift is an advance upon its predecessors.

Sixth Gift.—With the sixth gift, which is a cube of
the same size as the fifth, but differing in its *subdivisions*,
we complete the series of solid forms.

To understand these gifts we must clearly and definitely apprehend their *relation* to each other ; for it is this
relation which gives them their significance, and upon the
recognition of this relation depends the power with which
they are used. We conceive nothing truly so long as we
conceive it singly. It is only when the relations of any
individual object to universal law are rightly apprehended
that a clear insight into its nature is gained. Now, the
universal law of development is progress from the unli-
mited to the limited, from the homogeneous to the hete-
rogeneous, from simplicity, with its manifold adaptations,

to complexity, with its defined parts and restricted powers. Illustrations of this law are all around us. It is written on all inorganic nature; it unfolds itself yet more clearly in the plants and animals. Man, too, is no exception to

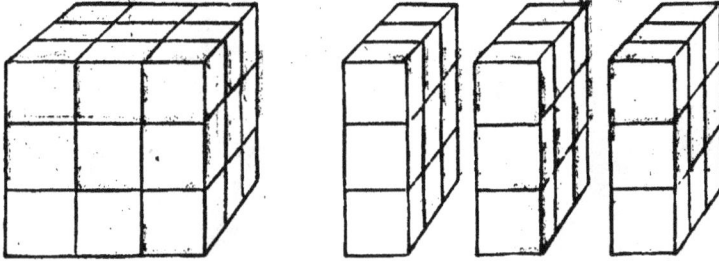

it, but physically, mentally, and morally progresses under the conditions which it imposes. Clearly, the law of human development should be the law of education; and the great originality of Fröbel as a thinker consists in his recognition and application of this vital truth. It was this underlying thought which determined in his mind the sequence of the six gifts just described; and any person who will carefully study them will find that there is in them a gradual advance in definiteness and complexity, and that each successive gift limits the freedom of the child, while vastly increasing his power within the boundaries defined.

Seventh Gift.—Education, however, must move not only from the simple to the complex, but from the concrete to the abstract. Hence in Fröbel's seventh gift we pass from the solid to the surface, and give to the child first *squares*, and then the different kinds of *triangles*. To preserve the connection of the gifts and to derive the surface—as, logically, it must be derived—from the solid, the square is represented as the embodied side of the cube. The right-angled isosceles triangle is then derived from the square by the diagonal line, and with this triangle as the standard of comparison the other triangles are also illustrated and defined.

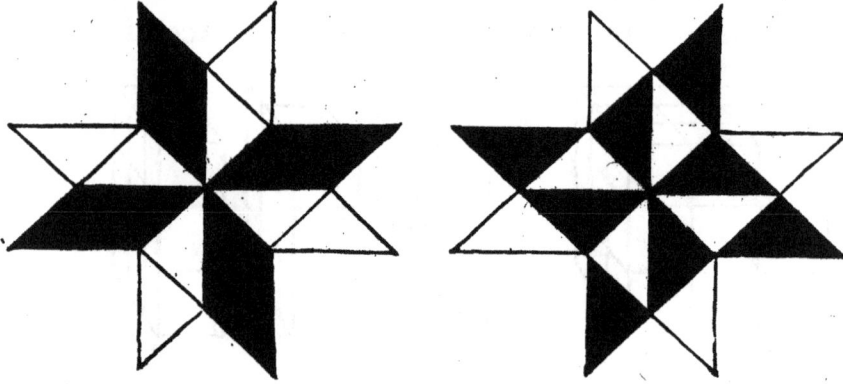

Occupation (8).—The interlacing slats form the transition from the surface to the line. These slats rudely represent the *line*, while, by breadth, they are still connected with the surface. They are succeeded by the sticks and wires which visibly embody the line, and through which the child learns to conceive the line as the boundary of a surface, just as he previously con-

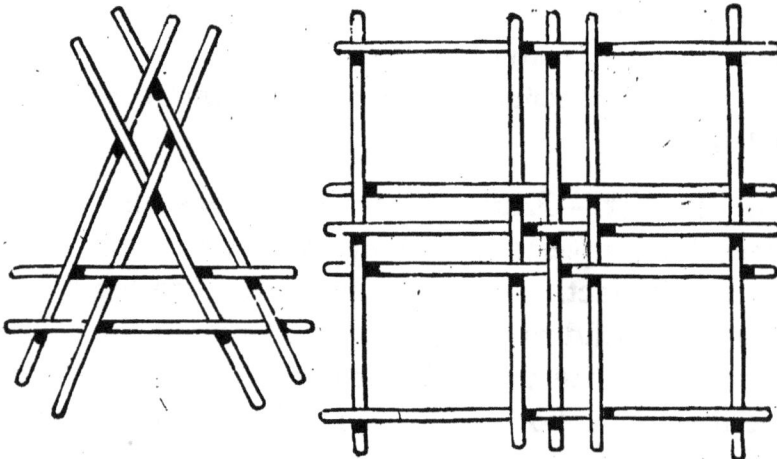

ceived the surface as the boundary of a solid. The limit of analysis is reached when we move from the line to the *point;* and in Germany there has recently been introduced into some of the Kindergartens the occupation of sorting, arranging, and combining into different forms small pebbles or shells, which are intended to represent the embodiment of the point. The sorting of seeds for the gardens also comes under this head, and with these crude material representations of the point is completed the series of the Kindergarten gifts.

I trust from what has been said that the following points with regard to these gifts have been clear :—

1. That the method of procedure by which the successive links in the series are obtained, is strictly analytical. Thus, by analysis of the solid we obtain the surface ; by analysis of the surface, the line ; by analysis of the line, the point.

2. That in using these gifts, the child effects no transformation of material ; he neither adds to, diminishes, nor modifies what is given him ; but simply classifies, combines, and arranges the elements he receives.

II. THE OCCUPATIONS.

Their Influence on Mental Development.— We pass now from the Kindergarten gifts to the Kindergarten occupations. But before I attempt to explain these, I wish to correct the generally prevalent idea that they are only mechanical employments, and that their purpose is simply to train the hand of the child, and to serve as a foil to the more intellectual exercises with the solid and plane geometric forms. The Kindergarten is not a school, where lessons are alternated with fancy work ; and there is no broad distinction between gifts involving more or less intellectual effort and occupations implying principally mechanical neatness of execution. The occupations of the Kindergarten are based upon the same general laws and regulated by the same general

principles as apply to the gifts ; and their effect upon
the total harmonious development of the child is even
more striking than the effect of the blocks, squares,
triangles, and sticks, to which they are sometimes most
injudiciously subordinated.

The Gifts and the Occupations compared.—
The true distinction between the gifts and occupations
is, that while the former are derived by analysis from the
solid, the latter are evolved by synthesis from the *point ;*
and while in the former the child simply makes different
combinations of definitely determined material, in the
latter there is progressive modification and transformation of the *material* itself.   Thus, from pricking, where
all kinds of harmonious figures are produced by simply
sticking holes in paper, we pass to the line in sewing and
drawing—to the transition from the line to the surface in
weaving and interlacing of paper—to the surface itself in
the squares of paper used for folding and cutting—to the
outlines of solids in pea-work—to the surface boundaries
of solids in the card-board modelling—and to the solid
itself in the modelling in clay.   Thus, by a different road,
we have reached our original starting-point, or rather,
having made a kind of spiral ascent, we are now survey-
ing the same truths from a higher plane.   A vital point of
connection between the gifts and the occupations lies in
the fact that the latter offer the child the best possible
means of embodying in visible and permanent form the
impressions received through the former.   Thus, in
pricking, sewing, and drawing, the children, when told
to invent, almost invariably begin by reproducing the
forms with which they have become familiar in their play
with blocks and sticks—the same truth applies to their
inventions in mats, paper-folding, and paper-cutting—

and an intelligent teacher can absolutely judge of the effect of her work by the free productions of her scholars.

General Principles of Technical Training. — Thus far we have considered the Kindergarten gifts and occupations simply from the stand-point of their effect upon the intellectual development of the child. They have, however, an additional significance in the fact that, taken together, they form a complete alphabet of work, and exercise the hand in all the technical processes by which man converts raw material to his use. Ever since the days of Locke thinkers and philanthropists have been trying to solve the problems of educating skilled labourers; and many have been the experiments of schools for the working-classes, nearly all of which have failed, because built on a wrong foundation. The truth which Fröbel plainly saw was, that the schools should strive, not to turn out good shoemakers, bookbinders, or watchmakers,— not, in fact, to teach any special trade,—but to give such preparatory training and practice as would make all technical processes simple. Upon this basis he organized the Kindergarten gifts and occupations, and, taken together, they represent every kind of technical activity, from the mere agglomerating of raw material to the delicate processes of plastic art.

Fröbel's gifts have thus a threefold purpose and a threefold application. Based upon the unchangeable principles of form and relations of number, they work powerfully in the direction of a healthy development of the mind ; by their countless beautiful combinations of colour and form, the æsthetic nature is roused; and by the practical work they necessitate, the senses are sharpened and the hand is trained. They appeal to the whole nature of the child, reaching at once his intellect, his emotions, and his physical activities, and contribute to produce a balanced development not attainable, I believe, by any other system.

So much for the Kindergarten material. A few words now as to the manner in which this material is used.

Handling and Doing essential.—The practical basis of the Kindergarten method is expressed in the formula, "We learn through doing." It was a favourite saying of Fröbel's, that the world is sick with thinking and can only be cured by acting; and accordingly in the Kindergarten free activity is the essential thing. The children roll and throw their balls, build with their blocks, and lay figures with their sticks; they fold, they sew, they weave, they model; and gradually the labour of the hand clears the thought of the mind, and by using objects as material for work their properties and powers are learned. In this lies the great difference between Pestalozzi and Fröbel; for while the object-lessons of the former appeal directly to the powers of observation, the latter realized that children would never carefully and exhaustively observe any object with which they were not practically occupied. Children in the Kindergarten observe because they are constantly trying to reproduce, and their failure to attain satisfactory results causes them to notice objects more and more carefully.

Advantage of Slow Progress.—Another excellent result of Fröbel's demand, that the child shall learn through doing, is that it effectually prevents that rapid acquisition of superficial knowledge which is the bane of the present age. It is true that the path of learning should be made pleasant; it is not true that it should be made so smooth that it may be trodden without effort. He who struggles up no Hill Difficulty will never reach

the Palace Beautiful; and the plan of constantly removing obstacles, instead of encouraging pupils to surmount them, both enfeebles character and destroys the vitality of the mind.

Self-dependence and Inventiveness. — In the Kindergarten the children work for what they get; but the steps by which they advance are so gradual that whenever they make a faithful effort they attain some result. Consequently, they gain faith in their own ability to surmount obstacles, and develop in mind and will at the same time that they are constantly adding to their little store of ideas and experiences. Again, what they know they must know thoroughly, for the mind can only use and apply what it has perfectly assimilated, and the salient feature of Fröbel's method is, that it transforms every element of knowledge into an element of creation.

"The Doctrine of Opposites." — If the practical basis of the Kindergarten is expressed in the formula, " We learn through doing," its intellectual basis is stated with equal definiteness in Fröbel's so-called Doctrine of Opposites. No feature of Fröbel's method is so difficult to explain as this, and yet it is the living link which connects the different parts of the system into a complete whole, and, as applied practically in the Kindergarten, is as simple in its nature as it is fruitful in its results. It is based upon the logical law of the identity of contraries, a law which many philosophers have recognized as the necessary condition of thought. We cannot conceive anything without implying its opposite. We cannot think *up* without implying *down*. We cannot think of *light* without implying *darkness*. We cannot realize *extension* without assuming *limitation*. "In all distinction," as has been well said, " the element effective of distinction works through negation, and, therefore, affirmation and negation, identity and difference, must be taken together as constituting between them but a single truth."

Fröbel claims that, as our thought is conditioned by this law, education should recognize and apply it; and he embodies it in the statement that "the principle of all creative activity is the reconciliation of opposites by an intermediate partaking of the nature of each of the extremes." This law governs the application of every Kindergarten gift and occupation; and while its philosophic basis can only be mastered by earnest thought, it is practically so simple that the child four years old uses it with the greatest ease and happiest results. The countersigns of the true Kindergarten are, " Reverse, and keep your opposites alike ;" and I feel sure that any person who will honestly observe the effect of this principle in the development of originality and creativeness will admit that Fröbel has found the true law of human activity, and has shown how it should be applied.

Physical Exercise. — A system based upon the necessities of the child must naturally provide for physical exercise and development. Accordingly, in the Kindergarten, gymnastic games, accompanied with song, are an essential feature of each day's programme. In these games the children get abundant opportunity for using their legs and arms, while the fact that nearly all of them are more or less dramatic makes them also favourable to the development of the imagination and sympathies.

The Social Element.—From the moral stand-point the chief significance of Fröbel's method is the recognition of the child, both as a distinct individual and as member of a collective organism. The great problem for man has always been, to harmonize the freedom of the one with the interests of the many, and to secure the development of the individual without sacrificing the order and stability which are the safeguards of general society. In the Kindergarten the children are associated together under the most favourable conditions, and while individuality is strongly developed each child early learns that his rights are limited by the rights of others. The only punishment inflicted is isolation of the selfish, wilful, or quarrelsome child from the society of his companions; and where, on the other hand, praise is given, it is given not by the teacher alone, but by teacher and children together. Thus the Kindergarten is a world in embryo—a world where small virtues are nursed into strength by exercise, where small faults are gradually overcome, because their effects are clearly seen, and where character is harmoniously developed, because the same truths realized as law are felt as love.

Progress of the Movement. — The results of Fröbel's system thus far have been partial and inadequate, because in many cases its principles have not been understood or properly applied. Its vitality and power are proved by the fact that through all discouragements it has steadily won its way, and every day challenges more imperatively the attention of educators. Planted now in all parts of Germany, made by imperial edict the basis of education in Austria, and introduced, though imperfectly, in Russia, France, Italy, England, and the United States, its merits will in the next few years be widely and thoroughly tested and the general applicability of its methods determined. Its advocates only ask that it may be judged by its fruits, and point to the children trained in accordance with its principles as their most convincing argument.

B

II.

FRÖBEL AND INFANT EDUCATION.*

(MISS MANNING.)

IN the year 1840, a German named Friedrich Fröbel, then near the age of sixty, established the first Kindergarten at Blankenburg, in Thüringen, not far from his birthplace. He was a man of simple, earnest character, with strong religious tendencies, self-observant, zealous in the pursuit of ideals, and extremely fond of children. After various vicissitudes, education became the one aim of his life. But he could not rest contented with existing methods; he saw too clearly their imperfections. So, making himself acquainted with the newest and deepest thoughts of Pestalozzi, J. P. Richter, and others on the subject, he amalgamated these with his own, and thus he became convinced of the truth of certain educational principles which, amid hardships, difficulties, and opposition, but with the help of a small band of united friends, he at length was able (at Keilhau and in Switzerland) to carry into practice. For many years these principles were applied by him only to boys of school age; but by degrees he began to turn his attention to infants, and this is how it naturally happened. Fröbel had from a child cared to search into causes and reasons. Therefore, later, when he saw any wrong condition of things, he could not rest till he had discovered some other wrong condition of which it was the result, and then he would ask, " Is there not some manner of proceeding, which, by attacking and altering the foundation of the actual state of things, may produce an effect that we approve, instead of one that we do *not* approve?" In this way he dealt with questions of teaching. His pupils did not grow to be as good or as thoughtful as he had hoped, or as their abilities seemed to promise. In his

---

* By MISS E. A. MANNING, *Langham Magazine*, May, 1876; and "*A Paper on Kindergarten Training*." (STANFORD.)

eyes they were crippled as to mind and character. Boys
came to him at eight, ten, twelve years old with defects in
their ways of thinking and of feeling which he could never
satisfactorily overcome. Looking, then, into causes, according to his wont, Fröbel came to consider whether some
change might not be effected farther back; whether, if children were carefully trained before the school age, they would
not profit much more by later teaching, and become better
and more useful men and women. The practical answer to
this question suggested itself to his mind in the form of
Kindergartens (children's gardens), and Fröbel spent the last
twelve years of his life in developing and spreading his ideas
about infant education. He died in 1852, not long after the
affectionate celebration of his 70th birthday, but his coadjutors
did not let his work drop. The system had already gained
a firm hold in Germany, and it soon extended to other Euro-
pean countries. In the United States it took root early, while
in England, after having been introduced here about twenty-
five years ago, and then being almost forgotten, it has lately
revived, and many persons of educational experience are
beginning to realize its value.

With regard now to Fröbel's principles of education, there
are two points to be particularly noticed :—1st, that his system rested upon facts ; and 2nd, that he carried it out in
accordance with the methods of nature.

First, I will refer to some of the facts which he took as the
basis of the Kindergarten system. Fröbel was a close and
accurate observer of children. When he taught boys, he
studied boys' tastes, boys' habits, boys' aims ; and when he
began to train younger children, he appreciated with marvel-
lous sympathy their winning characteristics, entering as a
welcome playfellow their miniature world, and treasuring up
in his memory their self-chosen modes of activity.

One of the most prominent facts that Fröbel observed is,
that a child is almost always at play. He meant by play
a joyous exercise of powers without any very definite aim,
and he felt that it is thus that children's vigour and power
manifest themselves and increase. The more we study young
children, the more we perceive that play is their only healthy
condition of existence. Repress playfulness, and let life be-

come hard and serious at five years old, what can be expected later but dreariness or frivolity ?

Another fact which Fröbel always bore in mind, is the child's delight in bodily activity. He loved to watch that merry practice of new-found strength, which leads to jumping, climbing, and scrambling, and the pattering of little feet up and down the nursery floor. By all this varied movement infants unconsciously give the necessary exercise to their growing frame, and learn by habit the difficult art of controlling limbs and muscles, while a quickened circulation promotes the due and rapid nourishment of every organ.

Again, there is mental activity, the first stir of wondering thought, as the child becomes aware of the sights and sounds around it, so new, so beautiful, so exciting. How it gazes at objects with its curious grave stare, and then catches hold of them, pulling them this way and that way, or tests their quality with its mouth, determined somehow to satisfy its inquisitiveness ! Fröbel noticed that the young child chiefly learns at first through touching and handling. As it grows older it supplements its own experience by questioning larger intellects. "What ? Let me see ! Why is it ?" and so on. Thus, by incessant eagerness, the infant acquires, in one manner or another, ideas of distance, number, form, colour, and texture, correcting in three or four years its original confused impressions to an extent that we cannot realise, and by means of such pleasurable exertion laying the basis for future mental achievements.

A fourth fact greatly dwelt on by Fröbel, is children's constructive power, the fondness for *making* something. Mothers and nurses often look upon this as a most inconvenient faculty. It certainly tends to the soiling of pinafores and the accumulation of rubbish, to the dangerous appropriation of scissors and knives, and even to the destruction of nursery furniture, and it usually goes by the name of *mischief.* But in this faculty with a bad name Fröbel saw the germ of that energetic activity which has crowned the world with works of grand usefulness and of mechanical power, and without which civilization would be impossible.

Closely connected with the desire to construct, is the faculty of imagination, which even in infants becomes the source of a rude but vivid art. Fröbel observed children's pleased attempts at drawing, the dramatic nature of their games, their insatiable love of stories, and he saw that fancy often leads them to discern more quickly the truer relation of things than we find easy with our more blunted apprehension. The influence, too, of music on children touched him intensely, whether as soothing turbulent passions, regulating impulse, or inspiring to happy exertion. Thus he found an appreciation of art and a power of invention already dawning in infant minds, and here also he partly formed his judgment from recollections of his own childhood.

The next point to notice is, that Fröbel believed in a moral and religious side of children's nature. He saw that before the age of six or seven habits of falsehood and obstinacy may have been acquired, the little boy or girl may readily have become selfish, grasping, and wayward. But he found that it was possible even at a very tender age to arouse sentiments which would lead the child to understand its relations to God and its fellow-creatures ; possible to train the conscience ; possible to call forth reverence, trust, obedience, unselfishness, and all good qualities of heart and soul.

I come now to the last fact which I shall mention, that children's life is naturally social. The eager delight that they show in each other's company clearly indicates that neither solitude nor living in continual companionship with elders is their normal state. Bring together children that have been moping each alone, and the friction of intercourse will make gladness flash from one to another of the happy party. And here I may add that Fröbel could not help seeing how naturally and how trustfully children associated with animals—what a close mutual comprehension seems to exist between tiny boys and girls and dogs and birds—and, indeed, with what ready sympathy their hearts flow forth into all the realms of nature.

Such, then, are the main facts upon the observation of which Fröbel built his system of infant training—the playful instincts of children, their physical and their mental activity, their constructive and their artistic powers, their moral and religious nature, and their social tendency.

It is easy to see how naturally the name *Kinder Garten* was adopted by Fröbel. In all his thoughts on education the illustration constantly present to his mind was that of the growth of plants. He used to say, "The tree is my teacher;" and he held the work of the gardener to be very similar to that of the educator. In an often-quoted passage he expresses himself thus: "As the farmer and gardener treat their seeds in accordance with nature, and in harmony with her laws, so we should educate the child and man according to their being, according to the inherent laws of life, in harmony and unity with nature and with the Supreme Being, Source of all life." The gardener imparts no force, establishes no laws, but, after making himself acquainted with the nature of the plants under his care, secures for them, by his watchful toil, plenty of light, air, water, and space, sure that the leaves, flowers, and fruit will appear in due time. And so, in the case of children, the teacher first acquires a true ideal of what they may become, and afterwards simply gives scope for the quickening and strengthening of their varied capacities. When then Fröbel had planned a training-place for infants, he called it a *children's garden*, expressing thus his educational principle, and conveying a beautiful idea of the kind of influences to be exerted there, such influences as may reasonably be compared to the sunshine, rain, and good soil by means of which plants thrive and grow. I may add that no forcing is consistent with his system. Open-air gardening he accepted as a comparison, but not the artificial methods which promote rapid results, for he knew that all healthy development is slow.

But Fröbel would have certainly failed in his practical schemes if he had not thoroughly understood children; and one cannot help being struck with the *wholeness* of his view as to their nature. He seems to leave out no characteristic, to forget no latent power. The child that he already trains in imagination is just the merry, happy, bright, inventive, active, loving child that every one delights to see. Himself of an affectionate disposition, he could sympathize with the desires and interests of the youngest minds; and when he was forming his plans of training he used to mix much with little children, noticing their ways with one another and the ways with them of their mothers and nurses. And, besides kindness and simplicity of heart, he brought to bear on the subject of education a keen and philosophic mind. He observed, not only children, but men and nations too ; and he found that facts in individual growth were confirmed by facts in the more extended growth of communities. He thought deeply on all human relations and duties, seeking everywhere for unity in variety, and for harmony through obedience to Divine laws. Gentle, thoughtful, poetical, and religious-minded, he was well qualified to show how children should be prepared for life, and I think it is rare to meet with any one who, as fully as he did, realized all their characteristics.

Of course, it depends mainly on the teacher whether a Kindergarten accomplishes its true intention ; and some of the objections that one occasionally hears raised against the system apply, I believe, to the many imperfect realizations that unfortunately exist. The important thing is, that a teacher should be thoroughly imbued with Fröbel's principle. No doubt she requires special training in the use of the gifts, and in the games and occupations, etc. But she will have studied these to little avail if she treats them as unrelated mechanical arts, instead of as helps to the carrying out of a whole ideal ; for Fröbel's system is, after all, *not* a system. It is life acting on life. It is the calling forth of the emotions, the intellect, the physical powers, and the conscience by one in whom all good faculties are already developed. The teacher must keep her principles constantly in view, and must test every portion of her practice by its conformity to that principle. Through a wise and loving influence she must prepare her impressible little pupils for further progress, and, if she has trained them as Fröbel meant them to be trained, they will begin their school-life with a happy and regulated consciousness of possessing force—physical, intellectual, and moral.

(From the "*Times*," *Dec.*, 1876.)

Mrs. GREY observed at the Society of Arts :—

"Of late Kindergartens have been coming into fashion. In all, little children would be found handling balls, plaiting paper, joining in games, and singing. Where the system is imperfectly understood all this amounts to nothing better than a mechanical kind of play having no distinct bearing on education ; but all these different occupations, when under the guidance of a skilful teacher, will be found to be co-ordinate parts of a profoundly philosophic system, each having its special educational value and all having a harmonious action and aim. Each is addressed to gradual and healthy development of a child's nature, and through them the child is learning, not only how to use his own faculties as tools, but something of the conditions under which he must use them, of his relations to the world around."

III.

ITS RELATION TO INDUSTRIAL TRAINING AND THE LIFE OF THE PEOPLE.

(MISS SHIRREFF.)*

IF I have succeeded in convincing the reader that the difficulty of introducing Kindergarten pupils to ordinary school-life, of bridging over the chasm between instruction through objects, and instruction through books, is one easily surmounted, and that the child who has enjoyed that early training will come so well prepared to make the best kind of progress in actual study, that it little matters though the latter be somewhat deferred—it will be evident that, as regards the cultivated classes of a nation, the groundwork laid in the Kindergarten is altogether advantageous. We have now to consider what it does for those whose position excludes them from later culture, and who must early in life be trained to industrial arts, or even be content with receiving no mental training at all after the years spent in elementary schools.

This is in one sense the most important side of the question, because affecting the widest phase of national life. Fröbel's system would still be invaluable, even if it were

---

* "*Principles of the Kindergarten System.*"

fitted only for those who will have the means of later culture; but it could lay no claim to being a system of true human education, because it would lack the element of universality, which must be the characteristic of the latter. This, however, is just what Fröbel's system does possess; it belongs to no class or nation, but to all. Wherever children are to be found endowed with ordinary human faculties, those faculties, moral, intellectual, and physical, are capable of being directed so as to ensure their harmonious development. No normally constituted human creature is incapable of being led to observe nature, to apprehend facts correctly, to exercise bodily activity and manual dexterity, to admire beauty, to love goodness, to revere God. Such direction, then, which is the aim of Fröbel's system, is a universal foundation of education; and it is further evident that the less chance any young creature has to share the treasure of culture hereafter, the more needful is it that this, which can be made a universal heritage, should be secured to him early.

Again, if the Kindergarten training can, as I showed in the last paper, facilitate the after-work of school, leaving time for other instruction, none can require it so much as those children to whom a few years of elementary teaching will be the whole of intellectual education, who must begin practical life at an age when other children are under tuition, and will ever after have scanty leisure to add to their small stock of knowledge. Every new facility for culture that can be given to this class is immensely more valuable than to the more fortunate minority, who can extend their education over ten more years of life, and can always command the best sources of knowledge, and the tuition that will make those sources available. In elementary education, therefore, Fröbel's system answers to a want that is daily more felt, as we strive too often in vain to cram the barest elements of knowlege into the few years the poor man can give to his child's mental improvement.

The children of the poor will not probably in a given time profit as much by the Kindergarten exercises as the children of more favoured classes, whose home habits have made good language familiar, have introduced them to a larger vocabulary, and given them the use of many things which may have refined the sense of touch and enlarged their perceptions; for as every hour of life is training the mere infant in one way or another, all its surroundings are, with or without purpose or method, influencing the future education; but this is only another reason why Kindergarten training is doubly essential to the poor child who depends for his entire mental culture on what he gets out of home.

Even if the required point prescribed by the "standards" has been reached, the boy is in a state of intellectual destitution that gives small hopes of his making any future use of his school acquirements. He has learned to read, but he has had no pleasure from knowledge. He has learned to write, but his hand is too stiff and clumsy to make the exercise anything but a laborious effort. He has learned to work rules of arithmetic, but he knows nothing of the relations of numbers, that give an interest to the dry ciphering. The possibility, as regards time, of including drawing in the elementary school course was, a few months ago, a matter of discussion at the London School Board, the difficulty already felt of meeting the legal requirements being strongly urged against such an addition. But Kindergarten pupils would come to school with eyes and fingers already trained for drawing, and, as I said above, with so much facility for the usual lessons that time may be spared for their other studies, bodily exercises, and manual arts, begun in the Kindergarten, thus completing the scanty teaching of the elementary school. Under such a system the labourer's child would acquire, in addition to the usual school learning, such a foundation of drawing, geometry, and natural history, so much habit of observing nature, and of inquiring into what he observes, that his working life would begin from an altogether higher level of intelligence. What his hand has to do, he will do with care and precision; what is before his eyes, he will observe with accuracy and discrimination; and what amusements he seeks, we may fairly hope will be beyond the pale of the public-house.

I have seemed here to speak of boys only, but of course the advantage is the same to children of both sexes. The girls so trained will in like manner carry the benefit of that more complete development of natural faculty into the work of after years, and as mothers they will take a very different view of their office from that which the women of the lower classes generally take. Remembering how early their own education began, and round what little things it seemed to turn, they also will begin early, and observe little things, and recall the Kindergarten songs as they watch the infant's cradle, and try to prepare it for the course of instruction which was so happy and so fruitful to themselves. The love of order and of beauty, which are such characteristic results of Kindergarten education, will nowhere produce more important fruits than in the women on whose care, and neatness, and regularity, is due everything that raises the labouring man's home above the sleeping and feeding-place of the human animal.

And now, if we suppose that the boy or girl on leaving school goes to learn a trade or any industrial art, it seems almost superfluous to dwell upon the advantage of beginning the apprenticeship with such command of the bodily and mental instruments of labour as Kindergarten instruction confers, with senses trained to accuracy, hands used to delicate operations, and the limbs to orderly and supple movements. It is evident that one so prepared would altogether distance another who has this necessary foundation of all careful workmanship to acquire. And as difficulties are lessened, the time required for learning a trade is diminished, wages may be earned at an earlier period, or leisure secured for further instruction. Suppose, for instance, the boy entering a carpenter's shop for the first time, and bringing with him a habit of observing, measuring, and drawing lines and angles, and of working with his hands quickly and correctly; is it not evident how soon the use of tools will become easy to him? Suppose him or his sister entering a china factory with eyes used to distinguish form and colour, having learned something of drawing, perhaps of modelling, and being trained at any rate to be true and accurate in all their work, what progress will they make, as compared with others to whom all this is unknown? Again, suppose they are employed in connection with machinery, what will not be the value of their early-acquired habits of order, regularity, and precision ?　Or let us follow the young girl to a purely feminine trade—to dressmaking, for example—and see how quickly her habits of delicate handiwork and correct observation will come into play ; how easily she will copy, how soon she will be fit to cut out, thanks to the childish exercises in accurate measurement and use of the scissors in cutting out paper designs ; or let us see her begin domestic service in common housework, where she will use her eyes and hands intelligently, and feel at once how beauty, as well as economy, depend on order and nicety ; or in the kitchen, where again the disciplined accuracy in work, the hand skilled in various movements, and the intelligence trained to understand the meaning of each manual operation to be performed, will come in to lessen indefinitely the difficulties of the practical training, and perhaps in time to persuade the public that what stands in the way of our having good servants is not popular education, but the want of education— that withholding knowledge will not increase the dexterity of the hand, nor give the qualities needed to direct it, and which belong only to carefully trained habits of observation and accuracy.

It is easy to imagine that many persons will say the advocates of this system ride a hobby, and that the large results we anticipate will be nullified, as the results of other plans of education have again and again disappointed reformers.　But the answer to this is twofold: first, no other system of nursery training is based on a philosophical study of human nature ; secondly, all other systems neglect two or three years of child-life, which the Kindergarten turns to account, and thus not only begin later, but begin when habits and inclinations are already in some measure formed, and probably hostile to those the educator wishes to train.　It is not so much that other methods fail, as that we are inconsistent in our expectations—we hope to reap what we have never sown. Those ordinary school methods teach certain definite things, and must be judged according as they succeed in giving accurate knowledge of them, but they do not attempt to draw out all the faculties, or to take hold of the emotional and imaginative side of the child's nature.　In short, the most complete instruction is not education, and the failures of the former cannot affect our estimate of the latter, which on any large scale has never even been tried. Now, Fröbel's system is education in the truest sense; to try it, therefore, is a new experiment in every way. It gives its most strenuous efforts to achieve those very things which ordinary methods neglect; it cares comparatively little for teaching, but it strives to fashion the human creature so that it shall derive full benefit from all later teaching, whether of books or the experience of life; and I repeat that its value increases in proportion as that later teaching will be circumscribed. To the great mass of mankind, whose lives must be devoted to bread-winning labour, the period of mental training comes not again after childhood is closed—in truth, it comes not again to any of us, though we may strive by later culture to remedy the shortcomings of early education. To the poor man those shortcomings are final, and fatally do they help to hedge in his whole after-life within the circle of bodily necessities.

IV.

THE ROOT-IDEA OF FRÖBEL'S METHOD.

(JOS. PAYNE.)

WE are still only standing on the circumference of Fröbel's expansive idea of education. Let us now enter within the circle, and make our way to the centre. In order to do this effectually, let us form a conception of the genesis of the idea —an idea not less distinguished by its originality as a theory than by its far-extending practical issues.

Let us imagine to ourselves Fröbel, after profoundly studying human nature in general, both in books and life, and minutely observing and studying the nature of children; in possession, too, of a large theoretical knowledge of education as a means for making the best of that nature; and, at the same time, impressed with a sorrowful conviction, founded partly on his own experience, that most of what is called education is not only unnatural, but anti-natural, as failing

to reach the inner being of the child, and even counteracting
and thwarting its spontaneous development,—let us, I say,
imagine Fröbel, thus equipped as an observer, taking his
place amidst a number of children disporting themselves in
the open air without any check upon their movements.

After looking on the pleasant scene awhile, he breaks out
into a soliloquy :—"What exuberant life !   What immeas-
urable enjoyment !   What unbounded activity !   What an
evolution of physical forces !   What a harmony between the
inner and the outer life!   What happiness, health, and
strength ! Let me look a little closer. What are these children doing ?   The air rings musically with their shouts and
joyous laughter.   Some are running, jumping, or bounding
along, with eyes like the eagle's bent upon its prey, after the
ball which a dexterous hit of the bat sent flying among them ;
others are bending down towards the ring filled with marbles,
and endeavouring to dislodge them from their position ;
others are running friendly races with their hoops ; others
again, with arms laid across each other's shoulders, are
quietly walking and talking together upon some matter in
which they evidently have a common interest. Their natural
fun gushes out from eyes and lips. I hear what they say.
It is simply expressed, amusing, generally intelligent, and
often even witty. But there is a small group of children
yonder.   They seem eagerly intent on some subject.   What
is it ?   I see one of them has taken a fruit from his pocket.
He is showing it to his fellows.   They look at it and admire
it.   It is new to them.   They wish to know more about it—
to handle, smell, and taste it.   The owner gives it into their
hands ; they feel and smell, but do not taste it.   They give
it back to the owner, his right to it being generally admitted.
He bites it, the rest looking eagerly on to watch the result.
His face shows that he likes the taste ; his eyes grow
brighter with satisfaction.   The rest desire to make his experience their own.   He sees their desire, breaks or cuts the
fruit in pieces, which he distributes among them.   He adds
to his own pleasure by sharing in theirs. Suddenly a loud
shout from some other part of the ground attracts the attention of the group, which scatters in all directions.   Let me
now consider. What does all this manifold movement—

this exhibition of spontaneous energy—really mean? To me it seems to have a profound meaning.

" It means—

" (1) That there is an immense external development and expansion of energy of various kinds—physical, intellectual, and moral. Limbs, senses, lungs, tongues, minds, hearts, are all at work—all co-operating to produce the general effect.

" (2) That activity—doing—is the common characteristic of this development of force.

" (3) That spontaneity—absolute freedom from outward control—appears to be both impulse and law to the activity.

" (4) That the harmonious combination and interaction of spontaneity and activity constitute the happiness which is apparent. The will to do prompts the doing ; the doing reacts on the will.

" (5) That the resulting happiness is independent of the absolute value of the exciting cause. A bit of stick, a stone, an apple, a marble, a hoop, a top, as soon as they become objects of interest, call out the activities of the whole being quite as effectually as if they were matters of the greatest intrinsic value. It is the action upon them—the doing something with them—that invests them with interest.

" (6) That this spontaneous activity generates happiness because the result is gained by the children's own efforts, without external interference. What they do themselves and for themselves, involving their own personal experience, and therefore exactly measured by their own capabilities, interests them. What another, of trained powers, standing on a different platform of advancement, does *for them*, is comparatively uninteresting. If such a person, from whatever motive, interferes with their spontaneous activity, he arrests the movement of their forces, quenches their interest, at least for the moment ; and they resent the interference.

" Such, then, appear to be the manifold meanings of the boundless spontaneous activity that I witness. But what name, after all, must I give to the totality of the phenomena exhibited before me ? I must call them Play. Play, then, is spontaneous activity ending in the satisfaction of the natural desire of the child for pleasure—for happiness. *Play is the*

*natural, the appropriate, business and occupation of the child
left to his own resources.* The child that does not play is
not a perfect child. He wants something—sense-organ, limb,
or generally what we imply by the term health—to make up
our ideal of a child. The healthy child plays—plays con-
tinually—cannot but play.

"But has this instinct for play no deeper significance? Is
it appointed by the Supreme Being merely to fill up time?
—merely to form an occasion for fruitless exercise?—merely
to end in itself? No! I see now that it is the constituted
means for the unfolding of all the child's powers. It is
through play that he learns the use of his limbs, of all his
bodily organs, and with this use gains health and strength.
Through play he comes to know the external world, the physical qualities of the objects which surround him, their motions, action, and reaction upon each other, and the relation
of these phenomena to himself—a knowledge which forms
the basis of that which will be his permanent stock for life.
Through play, involving association and combined action,
he begins to recognize moral relations, to feel that he cannot
live for himself alone, that he is a member of a community,
whose rights he must acknowledge if his own are to be ac-
knowledged. In and through play, moreover, he learns to
contrive means for securing his ends—to invent, construct,
discover, investigate, by imagination to bring the remote
near, and, further, to translate the language of facts into the
language of words, to learn the conventionalities of his
mother-tongue. Play, then, I see, is the means by which the
entire being of the child develops and grows into power, and,
therefore, does not end in itself.

"But an agency which effects results like these is an educational agency; and *Play*, therefore, *resolves itself into
education*—education which is independent of the formal
teacher, which the child virtually gains for and by himself.
This, then, is the outcome of all that I have observed. The
child, through the spontaneous activity of all his natural
forces, is really developing and strengthening them for future
use; he is working out his own education.

"But what do I, who am constituted by the demands of
society as the formal educator of these children, learn from

the insight I have thus gained into their nature? I learn this : that I must educate them in conformity with that nature. I must continue—not supersede—the course already begun; my own course must be based upon it. I must recognize and adopt the principles involved in it, and frame my laws of action accordingly. Above all, I must not neutralize and deaden that spontaneity which is the mainspring of all the machinery; I must rather encourage it, while ever opening new fields for its exercise, and giving it new directions. Play, spontaneous play, is the education of little children; but it is not the whole of their education. Their life is not to be made up of play. Can I not then even now gradually transform their play into work, but work which shall look like play?—work which shall originate in the same or similar impulses, and exercise the same energies as I see employed in their own amusements and occupations? Play, however, is a random, desultory education. It lays the essential basis, but it does not raise the superstructure. It requires to be organized for this purpose, but so organized that the superstructure shall be strictly related and conformed to the original lines of the foundation.

"*I see that these children delight in movement;*—they are always walking or running, jumping, hopping, tossing their limbs about, and, moreover, they are pleased with rhythmical movement. I can contrive motives and means for the same exercise of the limbs, which shall result in increased physical power, and consequently in health—shall train the children to a conscious and measured command of their bodily functions, and at the same time be accompanied by the attraction of rhythmical sound through song or instrument.

"*I see that they use their senses;* but merely at the accidental solicitation of surrounding circumstances, and therefore imperfectly. I can contrive means for a definite education of the senses, which shall result in increased quickness of vision, hearing, touch, etc. I can train the purblind eye to take note of delicate shades of colour, the dull ear to appreciate minute differences of sound.

"*I see that they observe;* but their observations are for the most part transitory and indefinite, and often, therefore, comparatively unfruitful. I can contrive means for concentrating their attention by exciting curiosity and interest, and educate them in the art of observing. They will thus gain clear and definite perceptions, bright images in the place of blurred ones, will learn to recognize the difference between complete and incomplete knowledge, and gradually advance from the stage of merely knowing to that of knowing that they know.

"*I see that they invent and construct;* but often awkwardly and aimlessly. I can avail myself of this instinct, and open to it a definite field of action. I shall prompt them to invention, and train them in the art of construction. The materials I shall use for this end will be simple ; but in combining them together for a purpose they will employ not only their knowledge of form, but their imagination of the capabilities of form. In various ways I shall prompt them to invent, construct, contrive, imitate, and in doing so develop their nascent taste for symmetry and beauty.

"And so in respect to other domains of that child-action which we call play I see that I can make these domains also my own. I can convert children's activities, energies, amusements, occupations, all that goes by the name of play, into instruments for my purpose, and, therefore, transform play into work. This work will be education in the true sense of the term ; the conception of it as such I have gained from the children themselves. They have taught me how I am to teach them."

V.

WHAT I THINK OF KINDERGARTENS.

(EMMA C. WHIPPLE.)

THE most striking contrast between the present primary school system and that of the Kindergarten consists in the utilization, by the latter, of the natural traits and activity of young children. Fröbel seems to have made the discovery of certain laws which govern the development of children, and to have, in the most wonderful, beautiful, and simple method, adapted means to this end.

The child is three years old, and may now attend a Kindergarten. We will, however, say here that the furniture and arrangements for a Kindergarten must have a special adaptation to this method of teaching.

The desks are covered with lines which make squares of an inch; this teaches the child to arrange his materials in an orderly manner; and as rules are given for each occupation, in a few days you will see the little three-year-old as intently counting the squares, to know on which line to place his blocks or sticks, as if he had been born to do nothing else. This enables the child to comprehend direction; "up" and "down," "right" and "left," are illustrated by means of these squares.

"But do you teach such abstractions to a child three years old?" perhaps you ask. "Is it not cruel to compel such a mere baby to sit at a desk and learn things?" Were this a primary school of the usual kind, this would be a pertinent inquiry, and it might, perhaps, come within the scope of the investigations of Mr. Bergh. But Fröbel has found that, by combining *knowing* and *doing*, a very young child is made capable of receiving *impressions*, which become by degrees the basis of *ideas*, and the chasm from the unknown to the known, from the concrete to the abstract, is bridged over successfully by the various occupations of the Kindergarten, and the instruction which the Kindergartener gives by means of them.

From the first happy hour that the child enters the "Paradise of Childhood," as the Kindergarten has justly been called, *hands* and *brain*, in *work* and *play*, preserve a happy equilibrium; and it becomes apparent to all who observe, that many a law of high significance to the child's future development has become a part of his consciousness, and that, too, without any strain of the mind, any weariness of the body, but with only the joy which *use* gives in the exercise of all the faculties given us by the Creator. Nor is the awakening of the religious sentiment in the child in any way neglected.

"How is all this accomplished?" you inquire.

Your little pet of three years, who has never passed a morning out of the light of his mother's eyes, has been deposited in the Kindergarten. The genial Kindergartener, whose skill has been attained through faithful study of her subject, whose tenderness thrills in her voice, and whose sincere love for childhood has led her to devote herself to this work, cannot fail to attract the little one.

Did you ever realize how much knowledge your child has mastered in the three years he has lived in our world ?

He has learned to walk, to run, to climb; he has learned to judge very correctly of the qualities of many things, and attaches a value to apples and oranges in direct proportion to their size. He is quite an adept in natural history, knows many animals, has learned to speak and understand the English language. He is withal an accomplished diplomate, and will " lobby through " a doubtful bill with a skill quite amazing and amusing to an impartial observer.

Now let us see what he is doing at the Kindergarten.

A card, with holes pricked at the distance of a quarter of an inch apart, is given to the little one, with a thread of bright-coloured worsted and a needle ; he is shown how to put the needle back and forth so as to form straight lines in series; he is told that these are " vertical," and when this lesson, by frequent repetition, has been fully taken in, he is shown how to form "horizontal" lines, and before you are aware that he has learned anything at the Kindergarten, he is using these terms intelligently in reference to objects around him.

At another hour a slate and pencil are given to the child, for the drawing lesson is in progress now. You will observe that the slate is ruled into squares of a quarter of an inch by lines cut in the surface of the slate, and here again vertical lines of one square's length are made. These lessons go on regularly, week after week, until lines of two, three, four, and five squares in length are made *perfectly*. This is the foundation for a system of drawing, so beautiful in its self-developing character as to seem to those who have observed it to be the only true method.

If you will look in at another time you will find your child and his little companions happily occupied with two, three, four, or five, or perhaps ten little smooth sticks, which they arrange, according to directions given, on the lines on their tables. When as much knowledge has been given as the young things may at once receive, permission is given to "invent" forms, and then each child starts off on its own hobby; the differences in the bent of each child begin to be seen whenever free invention is the order of the hour. The vivid imagination of the child will see a likeness to many things in the simple forms it can create from these few and simple materials; and—I speak from a careful observation of children under both conditions—there is far greater pleasure to the child in this exercise of its inventive faculties than can ever be obtained from the most elaborate toys, which are often broken by children, simply from the desire for material to work out their own inventions with. But our careful Kindergartener is ever watchful, lest even this occupation, so light, and rendered so cheerful from the orderly interchange of opinions and ideas among these inventors, should overtask the little ones. And now the luncheon, temporarily hidden in various tiny receptacles, awaits the busy little bees, and trooping they come; and, while the gentle and sympathetic care of the teacher makes an air of peace surround the little group, the luncheon is eaten, and rosy apple and golden orange, luscious grape or juicy pear, with bread or its substitutes, form a feast which seems a sort of angelic picnic; and happy merry tones bear witness to the healthful effect of the social feature of the lunch.

Lunch is over, the tiny baskets are emptied, the sense of satisfaction, which is inspired by food eaten in due season and in social surrounding, makes every one of good humour; and, the signal being given, the "ring" is formed, and *one* of the "one hundred plays" with the ball, which Fröbel calls "the earliest friend of the child," is played to the rhythm of a song adapted to each play. The balls educate more than mere skill of hand. They are six in number, of the three primary and the three secondary colours. Fröbel's directions are very precise as to the sequence in which these shall be used. A primary colour should be followed by a secondary colour, connecting it with another colour. So careful has he been in all that pertains to the education of the child, nothing is so minute as to be left unnoticed by him. Half an hour quickly passes, while "The ball comes round to meet us," "My ball, I want to catch you," and the ever-favourite play of "Who'll buy eggs?" are each played till every child has had a turn, after which more lessons follow.

You would weary of reading, sooner than I of writing, if I were to describe "the Weaving," "the Building," "the Pricking," "the Peas-work," "the Clay-modelling," and "the Folding" lessons which fill out the attractive rounds of occupations; and the object-lessons, which are given every week; of the knowledge of seeds and plants, which is imparted by sundry walks in autumn days to gather seeds of, perhaps, maple-trees, which are planted in pots, and are actually growing before their sight; of the bulbs, which were first made the subject of an object-lesson before they were started; and of the daily mission of watering the plants, which is given to the children in turn; of the visits to the fernery, where our frogs are passing the winter in serene and safe retiracy; of the groups of embryo artists, who are engaged at some portions of the morning in "freehand drawing" at the several blackboards. Indeed, I verily believe there *is* no limit to the delights of a *true* Kindergarten, kept, according to the teaching of Fröbel, by a teacher such as I have made my model in this letter.

I must not forget to say here that everything made by the children is set apart, from its first beginning, as a gift of love to "dear mamma," or "grandma," or "nurse," or some loved one; and one of the prettiest sights imaginable is to see these little midgets carrying home their completed works of art—a folded leaf, a pricked card, or a weaving leaf. Fröbel insists that the true way to learn generosity is by the *doing generous deeds*.

I have been for the past six months a daily attendant on the Normal Training-school for Kindergarteners. What I have in this imperfect sketch attempted to describe I have daily seen and have been part of. I cannot be considered as a youthful visionary. I am the mother of bearded men, and the grandmother of several grandchildren, and I have constantly felt great regret that my practical acquaintance with Fröbel's system came too late to be of avail in training my own children. My grandchildren, God willing, shall not lose some benefit from the late-acquired knowledge I have gained. If this statement of mine, which is a hasty picture of one day in Miss Kriege's Kindergarten, shall determine *one* mother to seek such a school for her children, or inspire some young woman with a love for the work of a Kindergartener which shall induce her to study the method theoretically and practically, I shall console myself for my inadequate description.

I must run the risk of making my letter tediously long by continuing to say, *that I do not think any person ought to attempt to keep a Kindergarten without a training under a skilled teacher.* For the aim is not merely to amuse the children and to keep them busy, or to make them imitate mechanically these occupations, but to truly develop their dormant faculties in all directions. Therefore a thorough knowledge of the scientific principles on which they are based is necessary in order to become an intelligent, conscientious, and successful Kindergarten teacher. The system of Fröbel is so beautifully developed, from its first principles, that a missing link would mar its harmonious completeness; and although for many years I had been interested in accounts of German Kindergartens, and had read with a strong predisposition in favour of the system all that I could find in English, I did not *begin* to understand the beauty of the theory, nor the happy adaptation of the methods, until I became a pupil at the training-school.

VI.

A DAY SPENT IN A KINDERGARTEN.

IT was my lot a week or two ago to pass a day in Nashua, N.H., on a visit to a friend, and while there, I improved the time by visiting a real Fröbel Kindergarten, a thing which I had long desired to do.

The foremost educators of the country have given their sanction to Fröbel's method for the education of very little children; and although the Kindergarten is well known by name, it is still quite seldom that one has the opportunity in this country to see the ideas of the great German edu-

cational reformer exemplified by a well-trained and thoroughly
competent Kindergartener. Many schools have adopted the
name without any knowledge of the system ; and their teachers, who have neither natural capacity, acquired culture, nor
proper training, are liable to do more harm than good, and
bring into disrepute the name which Fröbel chose, as most
expressive of his idea—Child's Garden—a garden where
little children are the plants to be trained and nourished
under the care of a faithful gardener.

We found Miss Held in a spacious room, sunny and
cheerful, the floor neatly carpeted, the walls adorned with
plants and vines and pleasant pictures of happy children,
and located in the central portion of the city. She was
surrounded by eighteen or twenty little children between the
ages of three and seven, sitting at low tables, the tops of
which are marked off into square inches. In their midst sat
Miss Held, thoroughly mistress of the situation, and the
impersonation of good sense and good humour combined.
Kind, helpful, earnest, patient, and devoted to her work, she
quickly wins the love and confidence of the children, even
the most shy, and they all seemed to know that in her they
had a very dear friend.

When we entered, the children were each engaged in
forming a pretty star-shaped figure upon the tables in front
of them, with coloured plane tables cut into squares and
variously shaped triangles. In this work they were guided
by Miss Held, who told them where to place each piece.
Each produced the same figure differing in colour. Each
was then told to produce such a figure as they might choose,
using all the pieces, and the result was truly wonderful in
the beauty and variety of the different combinations. This
is the method with all the occupations : first, the little ones
are led, then they are allowed to go alone. Then came some
very simple and easy exercises in drawing upon slates,
marked off in squares like the blackboard, from which they
copied their work. Then each made such picture as pleased
them best. In all their work they had the sympathy and
encouragement of Miss Held, praising when it was done
well, and helping on those who needed assistance.

After this occupation was concluded, folding doors were

opened into a room still larger, also sunny and bright, and the children marched in to the music of a pretty song, in which all joined. There for half an hour a series of games were played, uniting singing, simple gymnastics, and sport, to the intense delight of the participants, and the by no means slight enjoyment of the lookers-on. These games all have a meaning and an object, and are arranged with a view to the harmonious and healthy growth of the child's mental, moral, and physical nature.

After a short lunch the occupations were resumed. When they first gathered around the tables it seemed not unlike the assembling together of quite a number of ladies at a tea-party, the conversation was so brisk and sociable, but in three or four minutes each child was intently engaged sewing in and out with coloured worsteds. It was not like a school; there was no repression, no enforced silence, no fears of the raw hide or the teacher's frown, no books, no punishments; it was rather like a cheerful workshop where each was absorbed in his work, not as a disagreeable task, but rather as a delightful occupation. Strict silence was by no means enjoined, and if after a few minutes of employment a happy thought occurred to any little worker, he was encouraged to speak it out, and when any one was pleased he was allowed to laugh. While the rest were at work it occurred to one bright-eyed little fellow that he would like to recite a verse; leave was granted, and we undoubtedly got the benefit of his last exercise at the Sunday-school. A little girl followed with a verse that was evidently original, and none the less interesting for that; and then one volunteered a song. The charming innocence and unconscious simplicity displayed in their little interludes were fascinating. There was apparently no thought of showing off, nothing got up beforehand for the occasion, but they were spontaneous outbursts of their happy childish natures, mingled with an evident desire to do something that should meet with the approval of their friend Miss Held. Still the work went on and the beginning of very pretty designs was wrought out. The children seemed happy but not boisterous, attentive to their play-work, but not stunned into stupid apathy. It was order, and such order as seemed the outgrowth of the individual will of each child. And yet they had only been together two or three months at the longest, and most of them a much less time. How such order could be brought out of the chaos that must have existed on the first day is a mystery which one could hope to solve only after frequent and prolonged visits.

The occupations are varied every day, and we only regret that our stay was too short to permit us to see the " Building," " Weaving," " Folding," " Peas Work," " Modelling in Clay," and other works which they do.

We visited the garden, where each little one had his separate bed in which he could hoe and dig and watch the growth of his products to his heart's content. The spot was embowered in vines and several varieties of flowers, yet remained unharmed by the early frosts. One little fellow raised quite a supply of squashes and beets, and still another had obtained a wonderful growth of tomatoes. A real garden is considered quite essential to this system of education, and no Kindergarten is considered complete without one.

Fröbel thought education should begin at the first moment of conscious intelligence in the mother's arms ; he established schools for the training of nurses, and invented the Kindergarten as a bridge between the nursery and the school. It is not intended to supplant the primary school, but rather to prepare the child for it, and it is the unanimous testimony of the most accomplished instructors, that those who have had the longest training in the Kindergarten make the most rapid and satisfactory progress in the school.

VII. SOME DIFFICULTIES CONNECTED WITH KINDERGARTEN TEACHING IN ENGLAND.

THE introduction of Fröbel's system into this country is attended by some peculiar difficulties, to which it may not be useless to draw attention, in order that its friends may be prepared to meet them. They spring from its foreign origin, which makes its naturalization among us slow and troublesome. These difficulties may be classed under two heads, the want of teachers and the want of books; to which we may add a third, the reluctance in England to believe that considerable training and knowledge can be wanted for the teachers of little children from three to seven or eight years old. A few words, then, upon each of these points may be useful here.

The first difficulty we have to overcome is that of procuring Kindergarten mistresses; and with all due respect for the admirable foreign teachers who are working among us, it must be admitted that in order to popularize the system, to make it take root in this country, it must be worked by English women. Hitherto in most cases, when it has been desired to establish a Kindergarten, the difficulty of getting an English mistress has been the great obstacle. We shall never make wide progress till this obstacle is removed. The system cannot acquire vigour among us till it has a native growth; until then, it will be only as an exotic, needing care and propping up amid the free and hardy vegetation native to the soil.

Closely connected with this part of the work of the Fröbel Society * is that of using its influence to ensure that Kindergarten teachers are not only duly instructed in their special office, but that they are as far as possible well-educated women. The wider the culture any mind has received, the greater its aptitude for recognizing and acting upon philosophical principles; and conversely, the narrower the culture, the greater the incapacity for going beyond the rule of thumb, and often the greater the aversion to even recognizing that there may be something beyond it. In all departments of instruction it is essential that the teacher should not be a mere recipient and detailer of knowledge, that he or she should draw from a living spring, not from a rarely-filled tank; but in teaching little children, especially in using a method in which every detail is part of a connected, logical whole, it is more than ever necessary that the teacher should speak from a full mind, that her own observations or reading should supply her with illustrations, her own knowledge enable her to answer the questions which the children will ask, and which they will certainly not often put in the convenient form which will allow the answers of text-books to be given. The child's nature unfolds spontaneously, and the

---

* Hon. Sec., Miss Manning, 35, Blomfield Road, N.W.

teachers must be able spontaneously also to meet the requirements of that growth. The course of instruction for Kindergarten teachers ranges over so large an area that in itself it secures a considerable amount of knowledge. The best authorities are agreed that it should form a two years' course of study, the first given to acquiring thorough mastery of Fröbel's theory and of the occupations through which it is applied in teaching, and also that amount of instruction in various branches of knowledge which are requisite for the teachers ; the second to be spent in practical work as an assistant in a Kindergarten. Owing to the scarcity of training-classes, and the still greater scarcity of good Kindergartens in which the year of probation would be profitably spent, both these conditions are difficult.

Another difficulty arises from ignorance or prejudice, too generally prevailing in the English public. We are apt to be very impatient of preliminary study ; we want quick and ready methods, and are too apt to take an ill-made by-path for a high road to knowledge. We readily concede an apprenticeship of several years for a mere handicraft, but grudge half the time to that noblest of crafts which fashions the human creature for the work and duties of life.

A training-school for Kindergarten teachers has been at work for three years in Manchester, and certificates for first-class mistresses are given to the successful candidates after a two years' course of study and practice, and for second-class or assistant mistresses to those who reach a lower point of attainment. In like manner it has been decided that examinations shall be held under the auspices of the Fröbel Society for students trained in any of the different classes now at work, and for any others who may present themselves after private study, and wish to have their qualification tested. Certificates will be granted according to the result of the examination. An opportunity is thus afforded of taking some important steps towards establishing a standard of efficiency for English Kindergarten teachers, including the degree of general knowledge which is the necessary preliminary of all special or professional culture.

But it would be a great error to suppose that a teacher is fitted for her work by immediate Kindergarten training alone.

Fröbel's method requires much speaking, and a teacher must speak fluently and correctly, which of course she will not do without sound grammatical knowledge and habit of easy composition. Arithmetic is essential to Kindergarten teaching, and its peculiar method of making the children discover the principles for themselves could not be practised by one who was not familiar with the ordinary processes. As with the Arithmetical so with the Geometrical notions they impart, the teacher must be acquainted with the subject in its proper form before she will draw from the exercises with cubes and the drawing of geometrical figures all the lessons the children are made to teach themselves under skilful guidance. The Geography also should of course range beyond that of England, and especially include the elements of Physical Geography, which kindle the greatest interest in children to whom a common map is a dead letter. And in History and Literature some proficiency would be required, first, as the essential stamp of a careful education, and secondly, because few subjects so much contribute to enrich the mind, to furnish it with matter for illustration and knowledge of character, both so essential in the work of education. The fact that teaching is free in this country, *i.e.*, that no regulations prevent any ignorant pretenders from trading upon the equal or greater ignorance of parents, is one which does keep the general level of teaching power lower in England. There is no necessity of working up to a certain standard, and the best only, either of teachers or those who employ them, are able to fix a standard for themselves. But in a new and foreign system like this, in regard to which the public cannot but feel their own ignorance, the value of a certificate of competency is more likely to be recognized, and we may believe that teachers who do obtain such a certificate from a society that gives it only on the verdict of competent and independent examiners, will have a better prospect of employment than others whose work shall only have been certified by the teachers under whom they have studied. It is said that many elementary school-mistresses are studying the method and may come up for examination. This deserves all encouragement, and should be met by great indulgence in the examiners at this early period of our undertaking. The English part of the examination these mistresses will of course easily pass, or their Government certificate may perhaps be taken as exempting them from it ; their difficulty is an immense one—it is that of obtaining any sufficient knowledge of Fröbel's method through the medium of such scanty works as we possess in English, or of acquiring the elements of physical science which are indispensable for the Kindergarten teacher. One accustomed to teaching, and having had the training which that class of teachers alone obtain in England, would, with the help of good books, probably master the Kindergarten method without much difficulty ; but science is so deplorably neglected in our schools that the botany, physiology, natural history, and elementary physics, which are essential, will have to be studied for the purpose. Still, in our present condition, we must rejoice that any have zeal and courage to add this labour to their already laborious lives, and give a hearty welcome to their efforts.

Our object is, to inoculate the country at large with these new principles, and elementary school-mistresses will afford us invaluable aid, since through them we reach directly a very large class of children, and one for whom the Kindergarten is pre-eminently valuable. In the short school-life of these children there is no time for correcting the blunders of early training, while we may safely say that instruction given to them from seven to ten or eleven years of age would be profitable in a fourfold degree if their minds had been previously trained, as they would be in the Kindergarten, to observe, to inquire, to work accurately, and to live in orderly obedience and harmony. The whole nature of the child would come in a higher state of preparation under the influence of the ordinary school-master or mistress, and the short time they can command will be proportionately fruitful of good results. These considerations make us feel that every effort to introduce the system intelligently into elementary schools should be welcomed, and everything done to meet the meritorious efforts of mistresses who study in the intervals of fatiguing daily work.

We come next to writing as a means of spreading knowledge of the subject. I have said that the books are buried in a foreign language; but more and worse than that, they are separated from us by the strange invisible lines of foreign thought. Nothing is easier than to have books translated from one language to another, but far different is it to lift them from one region of national thought and sentiment to another; and yet this must be done in a subject like ours if we are to make real use of the valuable materials the Germans have elaborated for us. In matters of science and history, of classical learning or abstruse philosophy, in all of which the other nations of Europe have borrowed so largely from the Germans, the form of the thought as influenced by native associations and mental habits is of comparatively little importance, and minds habitually occupied with such matters are fit to deal easily with minor difficulties. But not only have *we* a difficult subject to study, but we require to *popularize* it. If we translate books, it is for the sake of the unlearned, of the young, who are necessarily unable to allow for national modes of thought, of the hard-worked teachers, whose scanty leisure for reading is heavily overtaxed if books are made abstruse by their method as well as their matter.

Yet we *must* get at the matter of these and other German works, for the knowledge we seek is there; and it is to be hoped that among the friends of the system will be found some good German scholars, persons able to imbue their own minds with the doctrines they present, and to give them to us, not in translation, when exact translation is unadvisable, but in a truly English form; in writings whose allusions and imagery, the associations appealed to, the actions and habits quoted in illustration, shall be such as simple English readers will feel and appreciate.

The literature of the subject now existing in English is poor in the extreme. Nor is the study of education itself made easily accessible to ordinary readers among us. We have in English many valuable writings on education—lectures, books, essays innumerable, and some of the highest value; and on moral subjects every point that the educator has to consider has doubtless been fully treated; but these books are often little known to the class of readers we must principally bear in mind. If we wish to make a study popular, to engage a large number of persons to take an interest in it, we must smooth the material difficulties at least out of their path, and not leave them to seek instruction in scattered writings, the immediate application of which to their particular branch of inquiry will not always be apparent. For instance, most writings on education refer to the school period ; and although principles are the same, the mind unaccustomed to inquire into principles will not carry back to infant life the psychological facts on which the education of a later period is founded ; still less will it be felt at once how much more important in an educational point of view is the period all such works ignore than the period they are exclusively occupied with.

This fact, recognized in principle by philosophical writers, is brought out clearly and in a practical form by Fröbel and his school only ; and therefore must these German writings be rendered easily accessible to English readers, if we wish their principle to exercise any wide influence over the English public.

LIST OF

KINDERGARTEN

AND OTHER

INFANT-SCHOOL MATERIALS

AND APPLIANCES.

SUPPLIED BY

THE CENTRAL SCHOOL-DEPÔT,

22, PATERNOSTER ROW, LONDON.

KINDERGARTEN GIFTS AND OCCUPATION MATERIAL.

CENTRAL SCHOOL-DEPÔT,

22, PATERNOSTER ROW, E.C.

THE FIRST GIFT.

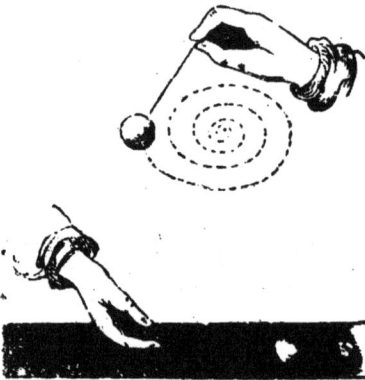

For the youngest children :

Six soft Balls of various colours.

Aim : To teach colour (primary—red, blue, yellow ; and secondary or mixed—green, violet, orange) and direction (forward and backward, right and left, up and down) ; to train the eye, to exercise the hands, arms, and feet in various plays.

A Set, in Wooden Box (*Fröbel's First Gift for Babies*). 2s.

DIRECTIONS for the use of the First Gift may also be found in **Laurie's Kindergarten Manual.** 1s.

THE SECOND GIFT,

Sphere, Cube, and Cylinder.

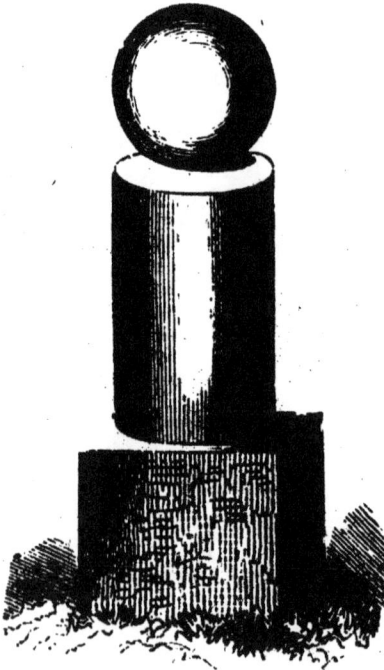

Aim : To teach form, to direct the attention of the child to similarity and dissimilarity between objects. This is done by pointing out, explaining, and counting the sides, corners, and edges of the cube ; by showing that the properties of the sphere, cylinder, and cube are different on account of their difference of shape ; by pointing out that the *apparent* form of the sphere is unchanged, from wherever viewed, but that the apparent forms of the cube and cylinder differ according to the point from which they are viewed.

The forms are of wood, machine-made for this special purpose ; are neat, and provided with the necessary staples and holes for hanging.

In Wooden Box, with cross-beam for hanging the forms. 1s.

For DIRECTIONS see **Kindergarten Manual.**

THE THIRD GIFT.

FRÖBEL'S FIRST BUILDING BOX.

Large Cube, divided into eight small cubes of equal size. Aim: To illustrate form and number; also to give the first idea of fractions.

In Wooden Box, 6*d.*

See also **Kindergarten Manual.**

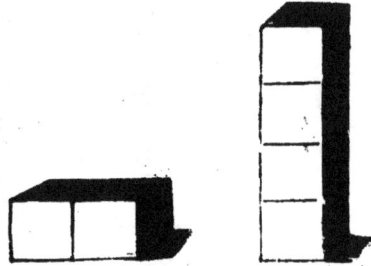

THE FOURTH GIFT.

FRÖBEL'S SECOND BUILDING BOX.

Large Cube, divided into eight oblong blocks. The points of similarity and difference between this and the Third Gift should be indicated.

In Wooden Box. 6*d.*

See also **Kindergarten Manual.**

THE FIFTH GIFT.

FRÖBEL'S THIRD BUILDING BOX.

This is a continuation of, and complement to, the Third Gift. It consists of twenty-one *whole,* six *half,* and twelve *quarter*-cubes, forming altogether *one large Cube.*

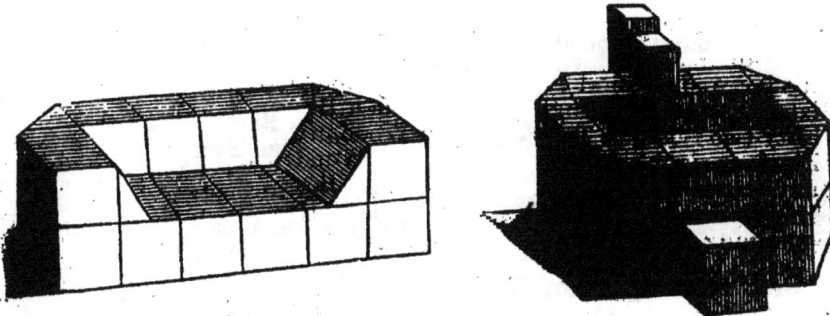

In Wooden Box. 1*s.*

See also **Kindergarten Manual.**

THE SIXTH GIFT.

FRÖBEL'S FOURTH BUILDING BOX.

This is a continuation of, and complement to, the Fourth Gift. It consists of eighteen *whole* oblong blocks, three similar blocks divided lengthwise, and six divided breadth-wise, forming altogether *one large Cube*.

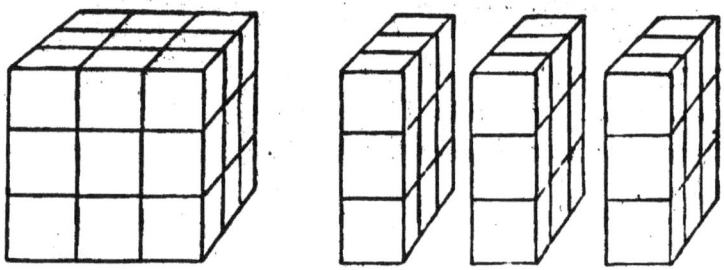

In Wooden Box. 1s.

See also **Kindergarten Manual.**

THE SEVENTH GIFT.

Quadrangular and Triangular Tablets of polished wood. These tablets, as well as the previous Gifts, are designed for instruction in reversing the position of forms and combining them. In the six previous Gifts the child had to do with *solids*; by the tablets the *plane* surfaces are represented; these are followed by the *straight line* in the Eighth Gift, and the *curve* in the Ninth Gift.

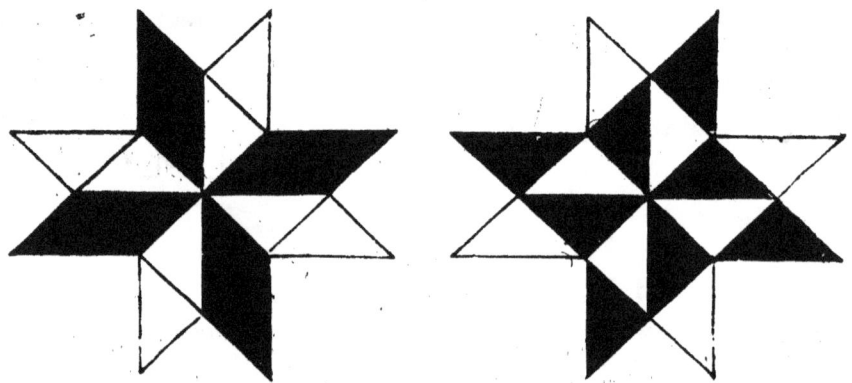

		s.	d.
A. Four large right-angled Triangles. In Wooden Box	... ...	0	4
B. Eight squares. In Wooden Box	... ...	0	6
C. Nine large equilateral Triangles. In Wooden Box ...	... ...	0	6
D. Sixteen isosceles Triangles. In Wooden Box ...	... ...	0	6
E. Thirty-two isosceles Triangles. In Wooden Box ...	... ...	0	9
F. Fifty-four right-angled Triangles. In Wooden Box	... ...	1	0
G. Fifty-six scalene Triangles. In Wooden Box ...	... ...	1	0
H. Fifty-six isosceles Triangles. In Wooden Box ...	... ...	1	0
Box containing different kinds of Angles (of binder's board) ...	...	0	8

See **Kindergarten Manual.**

OCCUPATIONS.

No. 8.

Folding Paper. The material for Paper Folding consists of square pieces, with which variously shaped objects are formed, and the elements of geometry are taught in a practical manner. The variety is endless, and prepares the pupil for many useful similar manual performances in practical life.

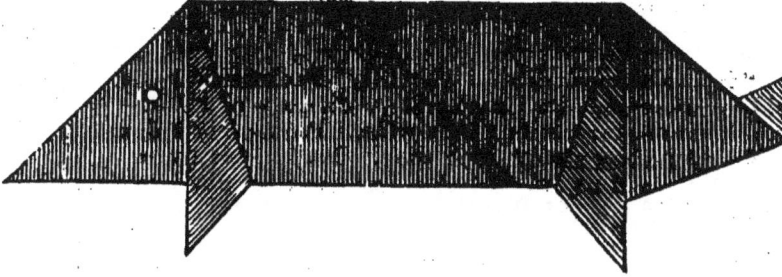

	s.	d.
100 leaves, white, 4 inches square	0	6
100 leaves, coloured Blue, Red, Yellow Surface, 4 inches square ...	0	6
100 " " " " ...	0	3
Diagrams to ditto, per packet	1	0

No. 9.

Cutting Paper. Squares of Paper are folded, cut according to certain rules, and formed into figures. The child's inclination for using the scissors is here so ingeniously turned to account as to produce very gratifying results.

Package of 100 squares, white. 3d. and 6d.

Package of 100 squares, coloured. 3d. and 6d.

Package of 100 squares, white and coloured, mixed. 6d.

Scissors for Paper Cutting. Per pair, 1s.

Gum, etc.

See **Kindergarten Manual.**

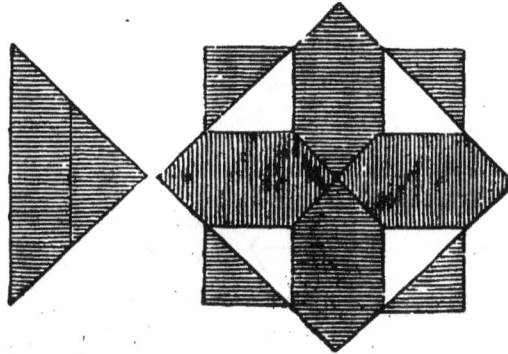

No. 10.

Weaving Paper. Strips of coloured paper are, by means of a steel or wooden needle of peculiar construction, woven into another (differently coloured) leaf of paper, which is cut into strips throughout its entire surface, except that a margin is left at each end to keep the strips in their places. A very great variety of designs is thus produced, and the inventive powers of teacher and pupil are constantly stimulated.

Mats, 5 by 6 inches, with slits and corresponding strips for weaving, slits ½ inch wide (No. 1). Package of 1 doz., of various colours.

Mats, 7 inches square, slits ¼ inch wide (No. 11). Package of 1 doz.

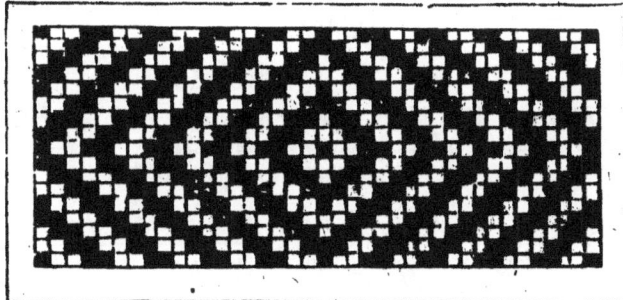

					s.	d.
Mats, 6 inches square, slits ½ inch wide. Package of 1 doz.				...	1	0
Mats, 6 by 5 inches, slits ⅓ inch wide. Package of 1 doz.				...	1	0
Mats, 6 inches square, slits ¼ inch wide. Package of 1 doz.				...	1	0
Mats, 6 by 5 inches, slits ¼ inch wide. Package of 1 doz.				...	1	0

(NOTE. Mats will be cut to order in quantities not less than 12 doz. of a particular kind.)

					s.	d.
Weaving-Needles of wood, per doz....	...	...	...	...	0	6
Weaving Needles of steel, per doz. ...	...	...	...	...	2	6
Material for Book-Marks, per package	...	...	...	...	0	6
Diagrams for ditto, per packet	...	...	...	...	1	0

See **Kindergarten Manual.**

No. 11.

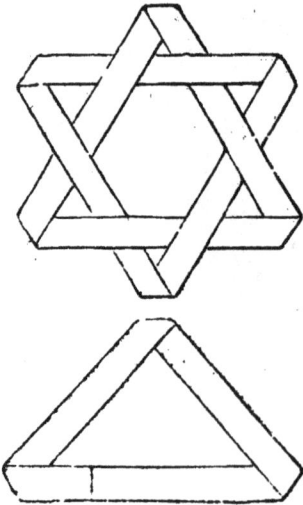

Intertwining Paper. Paper Strips of various colours, lengths, and widths, folded lengthwise, are used to represent a variety of geometrical as well as fancy forms, by plaiting them according to certain rules.

Packages of Paper Strips, containing 100 each, 4d.

No. 12A.

Plaiting. 100 Slats, 10 inches long and ¾ inch wide, for interlacing, to form geometrical and fancy figures, 1s.

Diagrams to ditto, per packet, 1s.

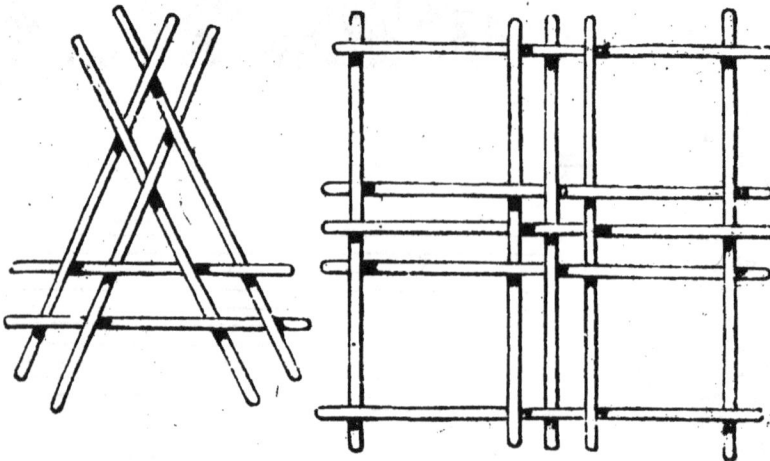

No. 12B.

A Set of Jointed Slats, with 9 links.

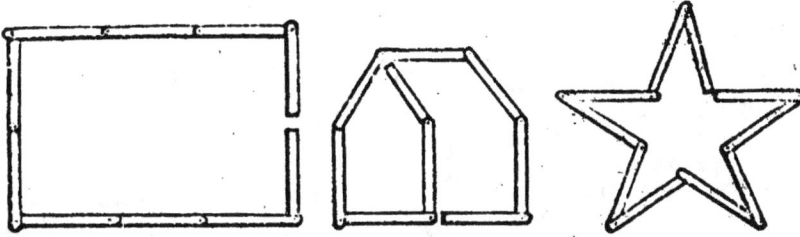

No. 13.

Sticks for Stick-laying. This Gift consists of thin wooden Sticks, about 13 inches long, to be cut into various lengths by the teacher or pupil, as occasion may require. These sticks, like most of the previous Gifts, are designed to teach numerical proportions and forms. Stick-laying is an excellent preparation for *drawing*. The Multiplication Table is *practically* taught by means of this gift. Reading, according to the *phonetic* method, is taught by imitating with these sticks the letters of the Alphabet. In the same way the Roman and Arabic numerals are taught previous to instruction in writing.

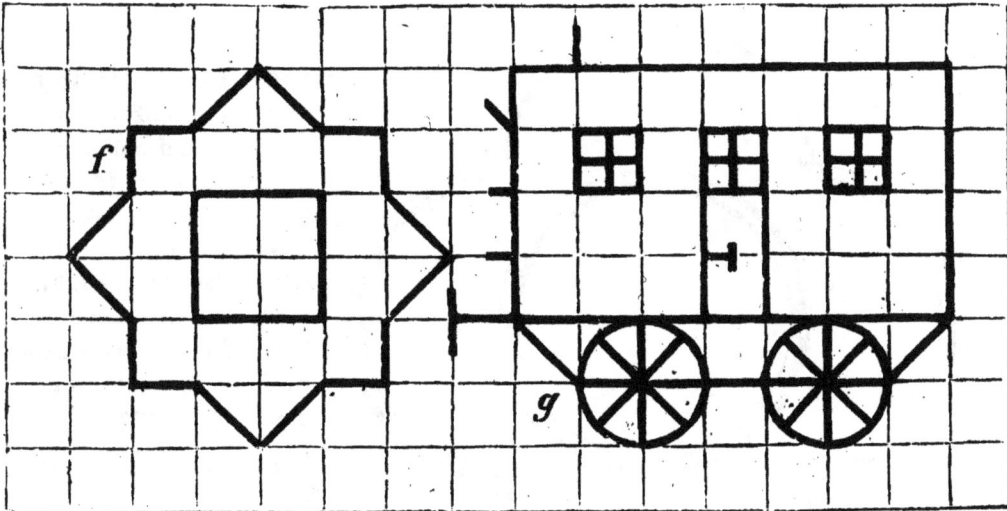

		s.	d.
Package of 500 Sticks, 2 inches long	... ...	0	3
Package of 500 Sticks, 4 inches long	... ...	0	6
Package of 500 Sticks, 13 inches long	... ...	0	9
Diagrams for ditto, per packet	... ...	0	9
Kindergarten Manual, and Pamphlet, No. 1, stick-laying		0	6

No. 14.

Peas and Cork Work. Peas are soaked in water for six or eight hours, and pieces of stick, of various lengths, pointed at the ends, are stuck into them for the purpose of imitating real objects and the various geometrical figures. Skeletons are thus produced, which develop the eye for perspective drawing most successfully.

In place of peas many persons prefer to use small Cork Cubes.

Sticks of different lengths, per Package (as above).

Box with coloured Sticks, and Cork Cubes, and Diagrams ...   . 3s. 6d.

Peas Work Box, containing Peas, Sticks, and Models 1s. 0d.

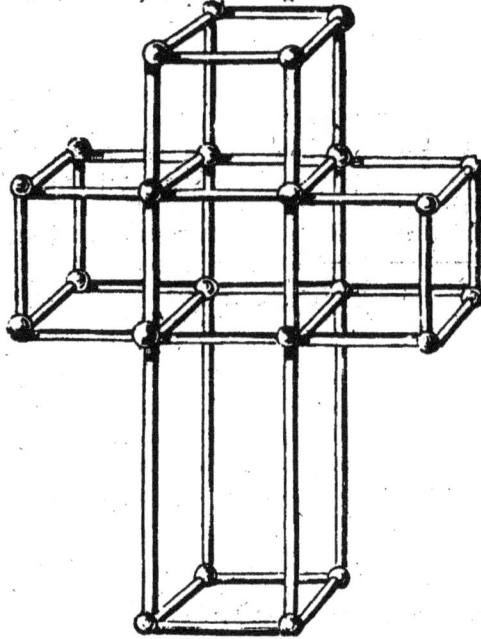

Diagrams to ditto, per packet, 9d.
See **Kindergarten Manual**.

No. 15A.

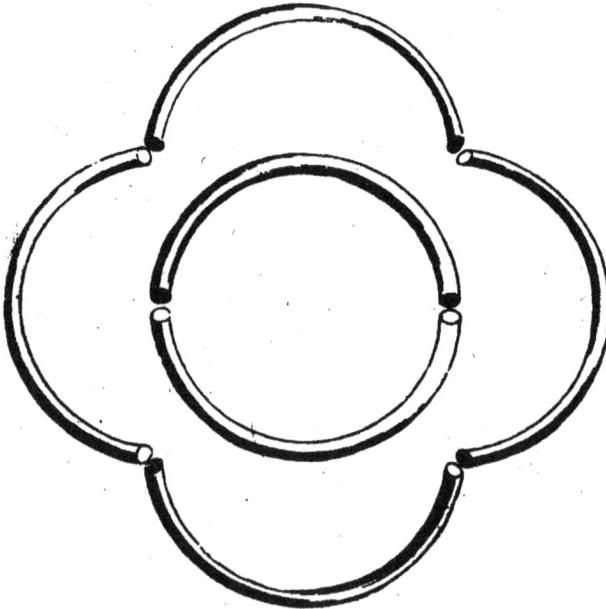

Rings for Ring-laying. This Gift consists of whole and half Rings of *various sizes*, in wire, for forming figures. These Rings, like the Sticks in the Eighth Gift, are intended to teach the first elements of form as an introduction to *drawing*.

Box of whole and half Rings of various sizes, 1s.

Diagrams for ditto, per packet, 1s.

No. 15B.

Thread-laying.——Threads 12 and 18 inches long.

No. 16.

Drawing on Slates and Paper. The material used is, first, *Slates* grooved in squares, next, *Paper* ruled in squares. This method of beginning drawing is the most systematic and perfect ever invented for young children. It is interesting to note how rapidly, by it, even the youngest pupils advance.

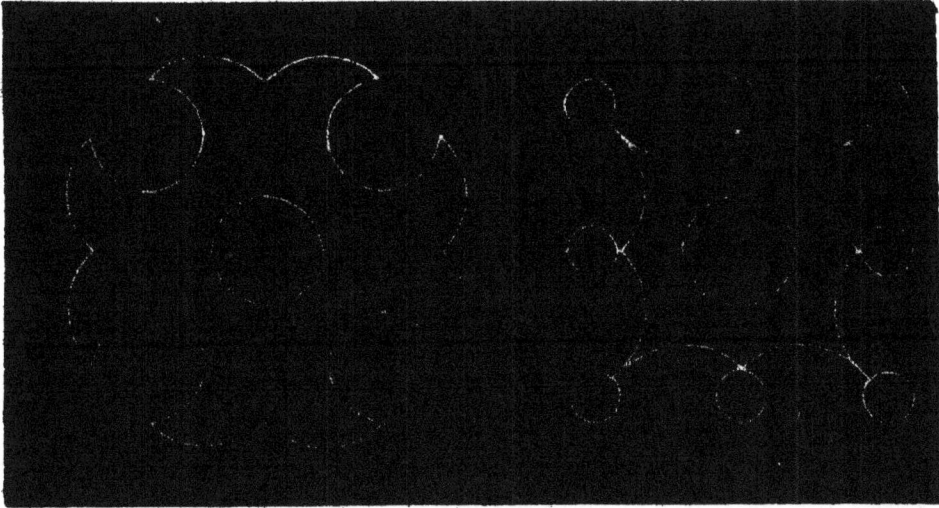

		s.	d.
Slates, Carbon, Unbreakable, ruled lines one side, squares the other. Unframed, 5d.; Framed		0	9
Slates, 8½ by 6½ inches, grooved in squares ... ... each		0	9
Slate pencils (fine), per doz., 3d. ... ... per gross		2	6
Slate pencils (common) ... ... per hundred		0	5
Drawing-Books, ruled in squares on both sides, each book containing 12 leaves, per doz. ... ... from per doz.		2	0
Drawing-Books, ruled in squares, post, on both sides ,,		4	0
Paper ruled in squares, post, per quire (24 sheets)		2	0
Pencils, per doz. ... ... from		0	6
Pencils (fine), per doz.		2	0
Kindergarten Slates, with Copies...		3	6
Diagrams, per packet		1	0

See Kindergarten Manual.

No. 17.

Perforating (Pricking) Paper.

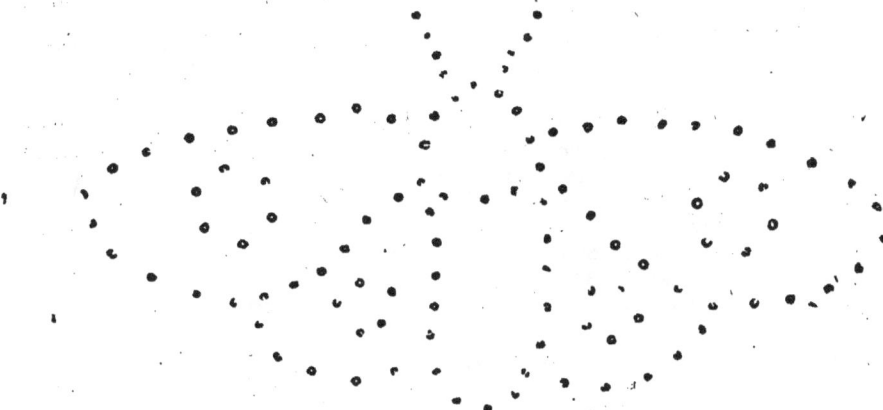

		s.	d.
Paper, post, ruled in squares *on one side only* ...		2	0
Perforating-Needles ...	per doz.	2	0
Perforating-Needles, with adjusting handles, and reserve			
points, in box ...	each	0	6
Perforating-Pads, white, each 6d.; coloured ...		1	0
Diagrams, in Wrapper ...	6d. and	0	9

See Kindergarten Manual.

No. 18.

Sewing. The Perforating Material is also used in this Gift. After the pattern is perforated, it is embroidered with coloured silk or worsted on card-board.

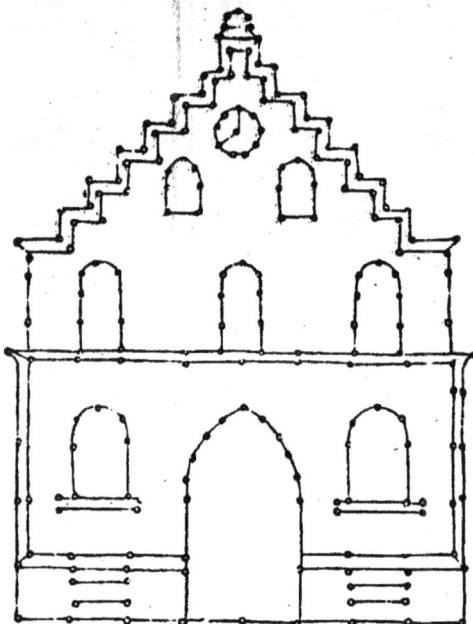

Pictures for perforating and embroidering, in 24 parts, each, 4d.

Card-board (fine), per sheet, 2d.

Twelve Designs, for perforating and embroidering, in Wrapper, Nos. 1 to 12, each, 9d.

Card-board (fine), to be used with these Designs, per sheet, 3d.

Card-board, perforated, 7 by 4½ inches, to be used with these Designs. Package of 6, 6d.

Card-board in sheets, in various colours, per sheet, 3d. and 4d.

Baskets for Cards or Needlework, embossed, for perforating and embroidering in worsted or silk, and otherwise ornamenting and making up, three sizes, 7, 8, and 9 inches wide respectively. Package of 6, assorted.

Worsted Needles, per doz., in Wrapper.

Worsted, 12 assorted colours, with 3 Worsted Needles, in Wrapper.

Embroidering Silk, 12 assorted colours, with 3 Needles, in Wrapper.

No. 19.

Painting. Painting for Children. A course progressively arranged according to Fröbel's System, for use at home or in the Kindergarten.

		s.	d.
Key Book for the Teacher, containing 12 plates of Coloured			
Designs, with explanations and directions ...		1	0
Exercise Book to correspond with the above ...		0	6
Primary Colour Box, for use with the above, fitted ...		2	6
Other Colour Boxes ...	from	0	6
Exercises in Colouring, consisting of Domestic Scenes, Domestic Animals, Wild Animals, Birds, Butterflies, Flowers, Small Bouquets, Rifle Costumes, Military Costumes, Landscapes, Ships, London Vehicles, The Young Artist, Scraps, The Young Colourist, Children, Geometrical Figures ...	each 6d. and	1	0

No. 20.

Modelling. Modelling Clay or Putty, worked with a small wooden knife, on a light smooth board, is used for the purpose.

		s.	d.
Modelling-Knives, of wood... ... ... each		0	4
Modelling Clay, per packet, 3 lbs.... ... ... „		0	6
Modelling-Boards, of wood... ... ... „		1	0
Patterns for Modelling and Drawing in Terra Cotta, each, 6d. ... ... per box		6	0
Vases, for same purpose ... ... from		2	6

BOOKS.

		s.	d.
Laurie's Kindergarten Manual		1	0
Fräulein Heerwart's Games and Songs (*in the press*).			
Guide to the English Kindergarten (Ronge)...		5	0
Kindergarten Toys and How to use Them (Hoffman)		1	0
Adler's Kindergarten Amusements. 12 Pamphlets, with designs in each ... ... each		0	6
Explanation of the Kindergarten. By Karl Fröbel		0	6
Hints on Introducing the Kindergarten System into English Infant Schools. M. E. Bailey		0	6
Sixty Kindergarten Songs, with Action		1	0
Kindergarten Music ... ... per sheet		0	6

Kindergarten Tables of various sizes. Quotations supplied on application.

Kindergarten Chairs.

Per dozen ... ... from £2 14s. to £3 12s.

[Packing and Carriage Expenses will be charged extra.]

The List on the foregoing pages comprises *only part of the Stock of Kindergarten Gifts, Occupation Material, etc.*

A very large assortment of kindred articles is on hand, and additions are incessantly made, both by importation from the Continent and by domestic manufacture, so as to render ours *the most complete and most extensive Repository of the kind in London.*

KINDERGARTEN MULTUM IN PARVO.

A Selection of Kindergarten Gifts and Occupation Material, suitable for use in Families.   In wooden box.   Price 12s. 6d.

CONTAINING:
FIRST GIFT.
SECOND GIFT.
THIRD GIFT.
FOURTH GIFT.
FIFTH GIFT.
SIXTH GIFT.
SEVENTH GIFT: 5 boxes of tablets (A.B.F.G.H.).
OCCUPATIONS: No. 8.
    Ditto   No. 9.
1 Chequered Slate.
2 Chequer Books.
3 Pricking Needles.
1 Modelling Knife.
1 Folder.
1 Box of Rings.
1 Pricking Pad.
1 Package of Paper, for Cutting and Folding.
4 Packages of Weaving-Mats and Strips, and 2 Weaving-Needles.
1 Package of Slats for Interlacing (50).

LAURIE'S
KINDERGARTEN MANUAL

OF

FRÖBEL'S METHOD

OF TRAINING CHILDREN FROM THREE TO SEVEN YEARS OF AGE.

Adapted from the German of FRIEDRICH SEIDEL.

𝔉𝔲𝔩𝔩𝔶 𝔍𝔩𝔩𝔲𝔰𝔱𝔯𝔞𝔱𝔢𝔡.

CONTAINING:

1. Systematic Order of the Occupations, by Fräulein Heerwart.

2. General View of the Kindergarten System.

3. Practical Instructions.

———

"KOMMT, LASST UNS UNSERN KINDERN LEBEN."—*Fröbel.*

ONE SHILLING.

𝔏𝔬𝔫𝔡𝔬𝔫:
THE CENTRAL SCHOOL-DEPÔT,
22, PATERNOSTER ROW, E.C.;
SIMPKIN & CO.; HAMILTON & CO.; KENT & CO.; AND
ALL THE SCHOOL SOCIETIES.

to form a figure;" but a certain latitude should be allowed in building; and if every form is exhausted, 2, 3, 4 to 7 cubes may be used.

74. **Further rule to be observed.**—"Every new form should be originated by the preceding figure." Any form built up, therefore, ought not to be immediately pulled down again, but by displacing or changing the position of one or several of the cubes, a variety of forms should be produced.

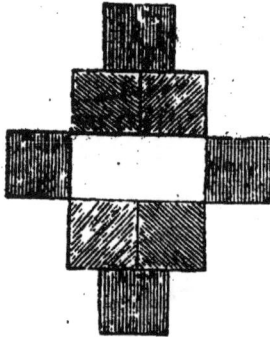

Fig. 6.—ARTISTIC FORM OF THE FIRST GIFT FOR BUILDING.

75. **Results in the development of the child produced by the third gift.**—By it the child exercises the whole of its mental faculties—its intellect, its fancy, its sense of beauty, and its powers of construction. It also *unconsciously* learns to understand the physical laws and their application; *e.g.*, the laws of gravitation and equilibrium, as exemplified by the hanging stairs, the cross, etc.

76. **Further observations.**—The child thereby is induced to express its thoughts upon everything represented by means of this gift; and to heighten the interest, suitable little tales and songs might be advantageously introduced; thus, on building a pigeon-house, a game at pigeons might be played, and the following might be sung :—

THE PIGEON-HOUSE.

R. KOHL.

The   Pi - geon house   we   o - pen   free, The

INFANT EDUCATION.

Descriptive Notes

ON THE

KINDERGARTEN SYSTEM.

EDITED BY J. S. LAURIE,

Formerly H.M. Inspector of Schools, etc.

1. GENERAL VIEW OF THE KINDERGARTEN SYSTEM: MISS S. E. BLOW.
2. FRÖBEL'S INFANT EDUCATION: MISS MANNING.
3. ITS RELATION TO INDUSTRIAL TRAINING: MISS SHIRREFF.
4. THE ROOT-IDEA OF FRÖBEL'S METHOD: JOS. PAYNE.
5. WHAT I THINK OF KINDERGARTENS: MRS. WHIPPLE.
6. A DAY SPENT IN A KINDERGARTEN: G. L. A.
7. SOME DIFFICULTIES CONNECTED WITH KINDERGARTEN TEACHING IN ENGLAND.

SIXPENCE.

London:

THE CENTRAL SCHOOL-DEPÔT,

22, PATERNOSTER ROW, E.C.;

SIMPKIN & CO.; HAMILTON & CO.; KENT & CO.; AND ALL THE SCHOOL SOCIETIES.

the standard of comparison the other triangles are also illustrated and defined.

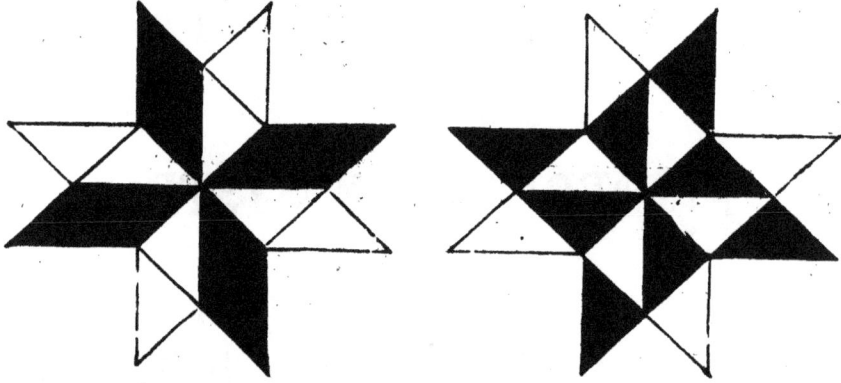

Occupation (8).—The interlacing slats form the transition from the surface to the line. These slats rudely represent the *line*, while, by breadth, they are still connected with the surface. They are succeeded by the sticks and wires which visibly embody the line, and through which the child learns to conceive the line as the boundary of a surface, just as he previously con-

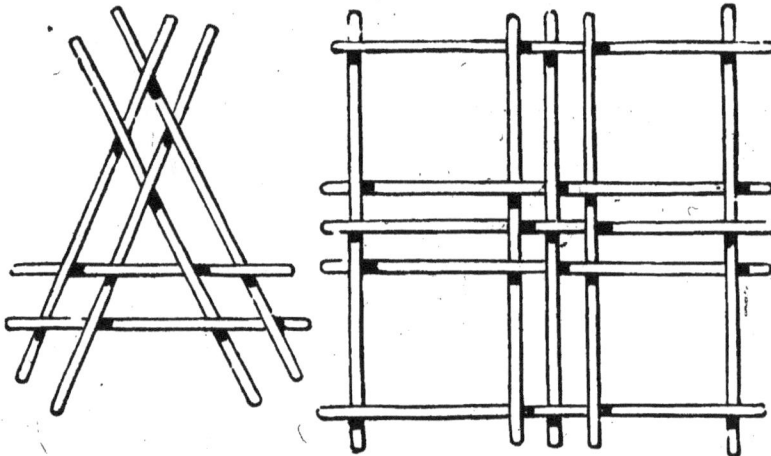

ceived the surface as the boundary of a solid. The limit of analysis is reached when we move from the line to the *point;* and in Germany there has recently been introduced